Credits

W9-BVL-817

For Heidi.

Mommus loves you.

Acknowledgments

t is one of life's great injustices that most books feature only the author's name on the cover and spine. After all, no title would ever make it to print—let alone into the hands of the interested reader—without the efforts of many others. In the case of this book, cover credit should be expanded to include Cindy Kitchel, Roxane Cerda, and Natasha Graf, whose expert guidance has transformed what was at best a rough idea into the book you see here; Lissa Auciello-Brogan, Henry Lazarek, and Donald Glassman, for their work laying out, proofreading, and indexing this title; and Jodi Bratch, for her fantastic photographs. To the many other talented and dedicated people at Wiley whose hard work has played a part in the publication of this book, thank you so much for your tireless efforts.

Credit should go, too, to the twenty-odd artists who contributed their amazing designs to this book: April Alden, Terry Border, Allison Brideau, Roxane Cerda, Michael Dittman, India Evans, Andrea Glick-Zenith, Kate Grenier, Debby Grogan, Yvonne Hoyer, Mark Kirk, Heather MacFarlane, Melissa Mazgaj, Tiffany Moreland, Mike Mossey, Melissa Nappi, Addie Panveno, April Richardson, Rebekah Seaman, Paul Siefert, Allison Strine, Lisa Vetter, and Shannon Wenisch.

And of course, friends and family members deserve heaps of credit for keeping me well and sane(ish), chief among them my smart, funny, and beautiful daughter, Heidi Welsh. Kid, you're the best. Thanks, too, to Ian Welsh, Barb Shoup, Steve Shoup, Jenny Shoup, Jim Plant, Jake Plant, the Pfeiffers, the Weitz boys, Sally Chalex, the DKG, the Friday Night Yogis (especially Rianne Keedy), Kate Bova and Miss Cole at The Flying Cupcake, John and Tim and Heidi at Hubbard & Cravens, and, of course, Fergus the Dog. I love you all.

Table of Contents

Introduction

The "Upside" of Recycling

n 1905, the year New York City began collecting garbage, denizens of that great city tossed out only 92 pounds of trash per person per year. Fast-forward to 2005 and that figure skyrockets more than ten-fold to a whopping 1,242 pounds. Think about that: New Yorkers at the turn of the last century threw away the equivalent of an Olsen twin in garbage. New Yorkers at the turn of *this* one tossed two and a half André the Giants.

So what gives?

There are, of course, any number of explanations for this dramatic surge in purge. Foremost among them is the simple fact that, for various cultural and economic reasons, New Yorkers of old bought less stuff in the first place than their 2005 counterparts, meaning they had less to dispose of. Second, the items those old-timers *did* buy were generally constructed to last and designed with durability in mind. Third, when an item's usefulness in its original incarnation expired, it typically found new life as something else—e.g., the shirt that simply could not be mended one more time was reborn as a cleaning rag.

Not so for the New Yorkers—or for that matter all of us in the Western world—today. Subject to the forceful and unrelenting currents of marketing, Westerners (yours truly included) are drowning in a sea of stuff—most of which will become obsolete in the foreseeable future because it will a) break; b) become overshadowed by subsequent product offerings; c) cease to be cool; or d) all of the above. Indeed, much of what we acquire is explicitly designed to be tossed after only a few uses at most—lighters, razors, tissues, pens, and the like. And of course, nearly everything we purchase is sold to us with such a surplus of packaging as to parcel up our very souls. Recent estimates indicate that Americans consume 60,000 plastic shopping bags every 5 seconds; 106,000 aluminum cans every 30 seconds; and 2,000,000 plastic beverage bottles every 5 minutes.

Of late, however, there has begun a small but powerful movement to thumb our noses at our society's disposable, consume-and-waste attitude. Spearheaded by environmentalists, the movement implores us to exercise what it calls the three Rs: Reduce, Reuse, and Recycle. Of the three, *Reduce* is the movement's most important directive. After all, if we do not buy something, then we need not concern ourselves with what happens to it after our need for it has expired. The second imperative, *Reuse*—spiffing up an item and using it again for the purpose for which it was originally intended—is likewise critical. The third edict, *Recycle*, involves pulping waste into raw material in order to manufacture new (albeit inferior) products.

Enter a fourth option: Upcycle. *Upcycling*, a term coined by William McDonough and Michael Braungart in their seminal work *Cradle to Cradle: Remaking the Way We Make Things* (North Point Press, 2002), can be defined as the repurposing of disposable materials (i.e. trash or other detritus) to create new products that are useful, beautiful, or both. Unlike recycled products, upcycled pieces retain—and sometimes even enhance—the look and feel of the original discarded materials. And unlike reused items, upcycled ones are generally used for purposes other than those for which they were originally intended.

This fourth option is the focus of this book. On these pages you'll find myriad projects that demonstrate how to make treasure from trash. As but one example, ponder the aluminum can that formerly contained your beer; it might be upcycled into a fetching pendant, the can's tab incorporated into an edgy belt, and the cardboard box that housed the can fashioned into a cover for a notebook. You'll also discover what types of castoffs work well for upcycling, and where to find them. If you're ready to see what goodies you can make with your garbage, then read on!

Part I

Funky See, Funky Do: How Discarded Items Can Take on New Life

Castoff Call:

I Love Trash and Why You Will, Too

What types of castoffs can be upcycled? Just about any—although, granted, some materials are probably best left in the trash (used hypodermic needles come to mind). Here are a few ideas to get your creative juices flowing:

- **Cardboard packaging.** Cereal boxes, beer cases, and similar packaging can experience new life as notebook covers, CD cases, envelopes, and the like.

- **Plastic bags.** There are a zillion ways to reuse the plastic bag you once employed to lug your groceries, store your bread, and pamper your produce—none of which include picking up dog poop. Instead, try fashioning them into a nifty clutch or tote. As for the doodad used to clamp your bread bag together: Why not repurpose it as a charm for a bracelet or some earrings?

- **Containers.** Sometimes a cigar box is just a cigar box. But other times it's a great foundation for a jewelry box, a gift box, or even a purse. Other containers—think coffee tins, oatmeal canisters, and the like—can serve similar purposes.

- **Glass bottles.** The beauty of glass is evident, even when said glass is designed merely to contain your root beer. Glass bottles are the perfect materials for any number of

Bottles are beautiful in their own right.

upcycling projects from vases to wind chimes and beyond. Plastic bottles, too, can be upcycled into an array of nifty items.

- **Bottle caps.** Bottle caps, which are groovy in their own right, can be fashioned into magnets, earrings, and more.

Colorful and interesting, bottle caps make great crafting materials.

- **Corks.** Why should the fun end just because the party's over? You can use the corks from your last celebration as fuel for myriad projects ranging from bulletin boards to bracelets.

Corks are an excellent project ingredient.

- **Cans.** Tin and aluminum cans make great fodder for projects, including candles, pendants, mosaics, and beyond.

- **Ephemera.** If your Great-uncle Morty has saved every issue of *National Geographic* since 1962, rejoice. You'll be rich in materials for upcycling when he finally decides to clean out his house. Ephemera such as magazine pages, sheet music, postage stamps, theater programs, ticket stubs, greeting cards, postcards, flashcards, wrapping paper, matchbook covers, maps, old books, wall calendars, and the like can embellish photo frames, bags, clocks, jewelry, and more.

Breathe new life into tired old books.

- **Photos.** Like ephemera, photos are natural choices for embellishing any number of items—but why stop there? Old-school photographers can find new ways to display their work by employing photo negatives in projects ranging from lamp shades to nightlights to bookmarks. Slide negatives, too, can serve many purposes—think notebook covers, mobiles, and more.

- **Toys and games.** Just because your Monopoly set is missing half its property cards doesn't mean it's "game over." A game's pieces can easily be transformed into charms for a bracelet,

Cans can be upcycled in any number of ways.

Board games contain loads of cool pieces that are prime for reuse.

necklace, or earrings. The game cards (not to mention regular playing cards) can become magnets and greeting-card decorations; and the game board can be transformed into a tabletop, a clock, or even coasters. Likewise, toys that are no longer in demand can be upcycled into any number of nifty knick-knacks.

Put those old odds and ends to work.

- **Odds and ends.** Who *doesn't* have a drawer full of castoff buttons, craft bits, beads, and assorted odds and ends? These doodads can serve any number of crafty purposes, embellishing bags, boxes, and beyond.

- **Clothes.** From sweaters to scarves, T-shirts to ties, clothes can be upcycled in any number of ways including bags, sashes, and cuffs.

- **Tools, hardware, and other manly stuff.** Just because the tools you inherited from your grandfather are as rusty as Britney Spears's lip-syncing skills doesn't mean you should chuck them. Tools and hardware make great wind-chime and sculpture components (as do kitchen utensils). Other garage/manly paraphernalia that can be upcycled include old license plates, electronics components, keys, tarps, and webbing from old lawn chairs.

- **Record albums.** LPs make great place mats, and can even be converted into bowls or coasters. Album covers can be adapted into notebooks or even used

Forage for Storage

As soon as you accumulate even a modest collection of materials for upcycling projects, you'll see the need for keeping them organized. Failure to implement some type of system results in chaos; unless you're an anarchist—which, given this book's demographic, you may well be—you'll go mad. Fortunately, you can channel any number of items you've retained for your upcycled crafts for use as organizational tools. Coffee tins make great containers for bottle caps, corks, and various odds and ends; cereal boxes are the perfect size for storing ephemera; Altoid tins, tic tac boxes, prescription pill bottles, film canisters, and the like work beautifully for needles, safety pins, and other wee bits; and cardboard shipping boxes can handle just about anything else. Plastic plates—the kind with little dividers so your kid doesn't throw a temper tantrum when his ketchup fuses with his alphabet chicken nuggets—are great for holding your supplies as you work (as are frozen dinner trays, deviled-egg and ice cube trays, muffin tins, sushi boxes, and the like).

Space Case

Regardless of what type of upcycling project you have chosen to undertake, you should take steps to ensure your physical comfort while working. In particular, you'll want to make sure your work space has adequate lighting. Also, ensure that your seat (your chair) has adequate cushion for your seat (your derrière). Good posture is also key. That's not to say you should work with a book on your head, but do make an effort to sit up straight. Finally, if you're like me, you probably don't have a lot in the way of brain cells to spare—meaning you should ensure that your work space is well ventilated, especially when applying sealants, solvents, and certain adhesives.

to construct boxes, carrying cases, and the like. LP adapters (the little doodads you or your parents used to play 45s on a record player) make great charms for jewelry.

What a Tool

If this were a book on, say, knitting or stitching or underwater basket weaving, a section on precisely what types of tools are required would be in order. But it's not. If upcycling is your bag, you might be called on to saw, snip, stab, sand, sew, solder, stitch, or staple—depending on what type of project you have in mind. This means that no single set of tools will suffice. Indeed, an upcycling project might employ any of the following:

Note: For specifics on tool requirements, see the "Materials" list at the beginning of each project in this book.

- **Power tools.** Drills, especially, are useful for upcycling projects. Also handy,

depending on the materials involved, is a grinder.

- **Hand tools.** Especially when creating jewelry or working with wire, various hand tools (such as needle nose pliers, round nose pliers, etc.) become critical. Hammers, saws, wrenches, and other hand tools may also prove useful.

- **Cutters.** Various types of cutters frequently come into play in upcycling projects. These include simple scissors, shears, paper cutters, wire cutters, craft knives (such as the X-ACTO brand, recommended for many of the projects in this book), tin snips, metal shears, and bolt cutters.

- **Household.** Some projects call for the use of household appliances, such as your oven, washer/dryer, and iron.

- **Sewing tools.** Many upcycling projects require the use of a sewing machine, along with other sewing accouterments (think thread, pins, seam ripper, etc.). At the very least, you'll want to keep some needle and thread handy.

- **Soldering equipment.** A soldering iron, solder, flux, and burnish tool are required for many types of projects.

- **Measuring tools.** A ruler and/or measuring tape will be required for many types of upcycling projects.

- **Adhesives.** Many products make use of a range of adhesives, from basic Elmer's variety glue sticks to rubber cement to hot glue to spray adhesives and beyond.

- **Sealants and solvents.** Your upcycling creations may occasionally call for the use of resin and sealants. (Note that you'll also want to have various paintbrushes and sponges handy for application purposes.) Solvents, too, may occasionally be required.

Who Gives a Scrap?

Where to Find Those Hidden Gems

If you have the good fortune of having hoarded decades' worth of ephemera, bric-a-brac, and other junk, then you probably don't need to venture much farther than your basement or attic to find materials for your projects. Ditto if you have a serious beer, wine, or soda habit. If, on the other hand, you have no pack-rat tendencies and are rarely thirsty, you may well be wondering just where you can find the necessary detritus for upcycling. In that case, this chapter is for you.

Embrace Your Inner Oscar the Grouch

Here are just a few places to scrounge for raw materials for your projects:

- Dumpsters, garbage cans, etc. If you felt an intense connection with Oscar the Grouch on *Sesame Street*, then you probably already know that one sure-fire way to land the occasional treasure is to sift through Dumpsters, garbage cans, and the like. For best results, scavenge in the more posh areas of town, and schedule your trash-diving trips around your area's garbage-pickup schedule. If you live in a college town, you can really hit the jackpot if you schedule a foraging run at the end of the academic school year. Be aware, however, that this type of scavenging is illegal in certain communities. Familiarize yourself with the law in your area before you begin pawing through other people's castoffs.

Note: Protect yourself from cooties when scavenging by covering as much of your body as possible—that means wearing gloves, boots, long pants (opt for sturdy fabrics, such as denim), and a long-sleeved shirt. Also, be sure to thoroughly clean any items you bring home before you work with them. If you're skeezed out by the idea of touching other people's trash, even while wearing gloves, limit your scavenging to any free-standing crates, bags, or bins outside the cans.

- Materials exchanges. Many cities boast materials exchanges, wherein businesses and individuals can donate miscellaneous materials specifically for reuse by artists and students, who can purchase the materials for pennies on the dollar. A few examples: Materials for the Arts (MFTA) in New York City (www.mfta.org); the Materials Exchange Center for Community Arts (MECCA) in Eugene, Oregon (www. materials-exchange.org); the School and Community Reuse Action Program (SCRAP) in Portland, Oregon (www. scrapaction.org); and Scrap Creative Reuse in San Francisco (www. scrap-sf.org).

- **Junkyards and architectural salvage stores.** For yet more interesting finds, visit your local junkyard and architectural salvage stores. You'll find all sorts of odds and ends, from large items that can be repurposed into furniture to smaller bits and pieces—think hardware, doorknobs, drawer pulls, and such—that can be upcycled into more delicate fare.

- **Tag sales.** Church rummage sales, garage sales, estate sales—they're all veritable gold mines for delightful detritus, especially board games, clothes, books, jewelry, and the like. (Peruse your local paper's classified ads to locate sales in your area.) The same goes for flea markets, thrift stores, and antique malls.

- **The Internet.** Odds are your community supports a Freecycle group. Dedicated to keeping good stuff out of landfills, Freecycle (www.freecycle.org) enables members to post items they no longer need in the hopes that other members can use them. All items are free, as is

membership. Other online resources (though not necessarily free) include craigslist (www.craigslist.com) and eBay (www.ebay.com).

Inspiration: The Remaining 1 Percent

So, okay, Thomas Edison totally had a point when he said, "Genius is one percent inspiration and ninety-nine percent perspiration." But that 1 percent of inspiration is pretty important when your brain is wholly barren of ideas. In addition to providing you with 30+ projects in this book, we've compiled this list of Web sites, craft shows, and publications with the express purpose of lighting your fire.

Helpful Web Sites Sure to Inspire

The Internet is one great resource for information and inspiration alike. Here is but a wee smattering of sites to get you started:

- **CRAFT (www.craftzine.com).** This companion Web site to *CRAFT Magazine* (itself an excellent muse) offers links to project tutorials that are sure to inspire.

- **Craftster (www.craftster.org).** Launched in 2003 as a repository for instructions for hip, irreverent, ironic, kitschy, and clever DIY projects, Craftster has evolved into a global crafting community. Special emphasis is placed on projects that involve upcycling.

- **Etsy (www.etsy.com).** Oh, God, how we love Etsy. Here you'll find thousands of beautiful handmade items for sale—as well as a platform to sell your own

11

Who Gives a Scrap? Where to Find Those Hidden Gems

pieces should you so choose. To spark your own creativity, try typing "upcycle" in the site's search field to see what goodies pop up.

- GetCrafty (getcrafty.com). Visit GetCrafty for how-tos, craft columns, and a vibrant user forum.

- SuperNaturale (www.supernaturale. com). An independent site devoted to DIY culture in all its glorious forms, SuperNaturale boasts an online magazine, a user forum, and a blog.

Books and Periodicals to Get You on Your Way

Sure, I like my own book best, and I hope you do too. However, that's not to say you won't be inspired by anyone else's. Here are a few titles that might light your fire:

- AlternaCrafts: 20+ Hi-Style Lo-Budget Projects to Make by Jessica Vitkus (STC Craft, 2006). Step-by-step instructions guide you through the creation of such items as curtains made from bandanas, a purse from a sweater, a bottle-cap locket, a shaggy rug from old T-shirts, a placemat from chopsticks, a snack-wrapper wallet, and more. That said, the focus of the book is on "low-budget" crafts rather than on using recycled items in crafting per se. (Although in some projects, discarded items are indeed repurposed.)

- Craftivity: 40 Projects for the DIY Lifestyle by Tsia Carson (Collins, 2006). The force behind SuperNaturale.com,

author Tsia Carson's Craftivity boasts a compilation of projects ranging from an embroidered screen door to undies crafted from old T-shirts.

- Decorating Junk Market Style by Sue Whitney and Ki Nassauer (Meredith Books, 2005). This book offers tips on finding good junk and repurposing it in interesting ways for the home and garden. Although geared more toward inspiration than perspiration, it does include step-by-step instructions for a few projects.

- Re-Creative: 50 Projects for Turning Found Items into Contemporary Design by Steve Dodds (Home, 2006). This title, written by a frequent contributor to ReadyMade magazine, contains 50 projects designed to transform trash—including old computer cases, soda cans, album covers, foam packing, and more—into useful home-décor objects ranging from clocks to frames to end tables and beyond.

- ReadyMade: How to Make [Almost] Everything: A Do-It-Yourself Primer by Shoshana Berger and Grace Hawthorne (Clarkson Potter, 2005). Written by the editor in chief and the publisher/ CEO of ReadyMade magazine, this title features step-by-step instructions, complete with illustrations, for completing more than 30 home-décor projects. Each project involves the use of recycled materials such as paper, plastic, wood, metal, glass, concrete, and fabric.

- *Recycle: Make Your Own Eco-Friendly and Creative Designs* by Moira Hankinson and Nicholas Hankinson (Kyle Cathie Limited, 2006). This title, geared toward repurposing scrap, salvaged, and other recycled items for use in homes and gardens, contains more than 60 "found-object," "round-the-house" projects. Step-by-step instructions and illustrations accompany most, but not all, projects in the book.

- *The Salvage Sisters' Guide to Finding Style in the Street and Inspiration in the Attic* by Kathleen Hackett and Mary Ann Young (Artisan, 2005). Inspired by everyday objects, the Salvage Sisters rescue 50-plus common castoffs—orphaned drawers, a hobbled couch, a broken birdbath—and transform them into style statements for the home. Alongside step-by-step instructions, the authors include helpful tips, alternative project ideas, and more than 125 color photographs.

In addition, check out these periodicals:

- *Adorn.* Devoted to hip, crafty ladies, *Adorn* is chock-full of projects and ideas.

- *CRAFT Magazine.* This magazine covers traditional crafting practices and techniques, but with a twist of technology, creative recycling, and innovative materials and processes.

- *ReadyMade.* This bimonthly magazine features DIY projects for smart, urban-minded, environmentally conscious crafters.

Craft Shows and Groups to Keep You Motivated

Craft shows are another great source of spark—especially when they're geared toward hipster types. Here are a few that fit the bill:

- Bazaar Bizarre (www.bazaarbizarre.org). What began in Boston in 2001 with a hodgepodge of friends attempting to sell their handcrafted wares has evolved into an annual extravaganza that, at the time of this writing, spans four cities: Boston, Cleveland, Los Angeles, and San Francisco.

- DIY Trunk Show (www.diytrunkshow.com). Chicago-area upcyclers flock to this annual event, which features the best of the area's alternative craft community.

- Maker Faire (www.makerfaire.com). Maker Faire, held twice annually (once in Austin, Texas, and once in the San Francisco Bay Area), celebrates arts, crafts, engineering, science, and the DIY lifestyle, drawing legions of techies, teachers, students, tinkerers, inventors, and, yes, crafters. Performances, demonstrations, and hands-on activities make this event family-friendly and fun.

- Renegade Craft Fair (www.renegadecraft.com). Launched in 2003, the Renegade Craft Fair now occurs twice annually—once in Chicago and once in Brooklyn. Both venues boast more than 150 vendors, making them destinations for crafties from all over the country.

If meeting fellow crafters helps crank your motor, look into joining a local crafting group—modern versions of the sewing circles or quilting bees of old. Here are a couple of places to start your search:

- **Church of Craft (churchofcraft.org).** With "parishes" in nine cities worldwide, this church is devoted to spreading the word of craft. Regular "craft-ons" allow members a chance to congregate and commune.

- **Craft Mafia (craftmafia.com).** This crafting famiglia, founded in 2003 in Austin, Texas, now spans 36 cities from Louisville to Lubbock to Leeds. If your community does not yet harbor a chapter of the Craft Mafia, you can start your own.

Part
II

Waste Not Want Not: Creating Objects of Desire

Diamonds in the Rough:

Making Jewelry from Junk

Can-Do Attitude

Designer: Shannon Wenisch

If recyclables were subject to the same inane categorizations as high school graduates, aluminum cans would surely be "Most Popular." That's because more than 50 percent of all aluminum cans are recycled. Of course, the flip side of this statistic is that 50 percent of all aluminum cans *aren't* recycled, meaning there are plenty left over for crafts such as this pendant, fashioned from an Arizona Iced Tea can.

MATERIALS:

- An aluminum can (We used an Arizona Iced Tea can.)
- Tin snips
- Ruler
- Heavy-duty scissors
- Masking tape
- Small paintbrush
- Black permanent marker
- Work gloves
- Sandpaper
- Spray adhesive
- 1 sheet ⅛-in. thick balsa wood or basswood
- Resin and hardener (We used EnviroTex Lite.)
- Small plastic cup or container
- Wooden stir stick
- 2 bamboo skewers
- Bowl
- Drill and 1/16-in. drill bit
- 1 jump ring

Instructions

1 Use your tin snips to cut the top and bottom ends off the can, such that you are left with an aluminum cylinder.

Note: Unless you want to slice off a digit or two in the process, make sure you wear work gloves when cutting.

2 Still using your tin snips and work gloves, cut the cylinder in a straight line lengthwise and unfurl it, resulting in an aluminum rectangle.

3 Flatten out the aluminum rectangle as much as possible by gently working it with your hands.

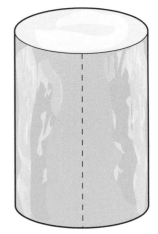

Step 2: Cut the can and unfurl it to create an aluminum rectangle.

4   Determine which part of the can you want to use for your pendant. Then, using the ruler and the permanent marker, mark the portion of the can you will cut.

Tip: Try taping down the edges of the aluminum rectangle on a flat surface before you mark it up; this will help to keep it straight.

5   Again using the tin snips (did we mention the gloves?), cut out the marked piece of aluminum, ensuring that it is flat.

6   Channeling your inner Tony Soprano, use sandpaper to rough up the back of the piece of aluminum you just cut.

7   Apply spray adhesive to the back of the aluminum and to your sheet of balsa wood or basswood.

Note: Don't worry about cutting the wood down to size to match the aluminum just yet. You'll do that in a bit.

8   Adhere your piece of aluminum to the wood and smooth it out. (You may need to wait a moment for the spray adhesive to become tacky; see the adhesive's instructions for details.)

9   Using your heavy-duty scissors, cut the wood around the aluminum piece. Be careful here—the wood may split along the grain, so go slowly.

10 Using the sandpaper, dull the sharp corners and smooth the sides of the pendant.

11 With the black permanent marker, color the sides and back of the wood for a more finished look.

12 In a well-ventilated area, use a wooden stir stick to mix the resin and hardener in a small plastic container. (Follow the manufacturer's instructions carefully to ensure the resin will harden properly.) You don't need much; just enough to cover the top and sides of the pendant.

13 Place 2 bamboo skewers in parallel on a level, protected surface, and lay the pendant on the skewers. (This will prevent the pendant from sticking to the surface.)

14 Using a small paintbrush, apply a very thin layer of the resin/hardener compound to the edges of the pendant. Don't use too much; otherwise, you'll wind up with drips, and the pendant will stick to the skewers.

15 Pour a very small amount of the resin/hardener compound on the top surface of the pendant. Use just enough to cover the top; don't let the compound drip down the sides. The surface tension in the liquid should help prevent runoff down the edges.

16 Using the stir stick, spread the resin to distribute it evenly on the top of the pendant.

17 Gently exhale on the surface of the pendant to help eliminate bubbles in the resin.

18 Cover the pendant with a bowl to prevent dust particles from settling on the resin and allow it to dry. (This usually takes 3 days.)

19 After the top surface of the pendant has dried, flip the pendant over and repeat steps 15–18.

20 Drill a hole close to the top of the pendant.

21 Feed a jump ring through the hole you drilled and attach the pendant to the chain or cord of your choice.

Good Credit

Designer: Roxane Cerda

Since the average American has, like, 4 bazillion expired, spare, or junk-mail credit cards lying around, turning them into something useful is both resourceful and space-saving. One idea: Snip them into small tiles and link them together to form a fabulous cuff that's also super light-weight.

MATERIALS:

- 3 or more credit cards
- Fine-point permanent marker
- Ruler
- Scissors
- Small scrap of spare, thin cardboard (like from a food box)
- Nail file

- China marker
- Sturdy X-ACTO knife
- Drill with 1/32-in. bit
- 12 7mm jump rings
- 8-strand slide clasp (or any multistrand clasp that is 1 1/4 in. or longer)
- Needle nose pliers

Instructions

1 Using your permanent marker and ruler, mark a ¾ × ⅝-in. rectangle on a small piece of spare cardboard.

2 Using your scissors, cut out the rectangle, rounding the edges slightly so that the shape of the finished piece resembles that of a very small credit card. This will be your template for cutting out the tiles.

3 Position your template over a portion of your credit card that has interesting colors, designs, or funky images, and trace around the template with the permanent marker.

4 Repeat step 3 26 more times, marking a total of 27 tiles.

Note: This makes an 8 to 8½-in. bracelet. For those of you with smaller wrists, mark 21 tiles for a 6½-in. bracelet or 24 tiles for a 7½-in. bracelet.

5 Using your scissors, cut out each of the pieces.

6 Smooth any rough edges on each tile using the nail file.

7 Arrange the tiles in a grid pattern, with each column in the grid containing 3 tiles and each row containing 9 tiles. Play around with the arrangement until you have the look you want. The tiles in the middle of the arrangement will be on the top of your wrist, so if you have a particular favorite, consider positioning it in the center.

Note: The number of tiles in each row will be different if you cut only 21 or 24 in order to create a smaller bracelet.

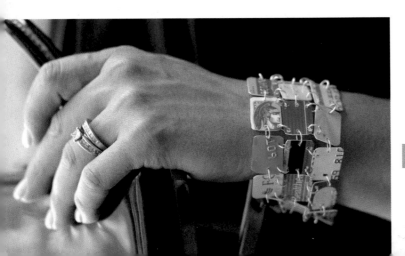

8 Using the China marker, number the backside of each tile so that you can assemble the bracelet in order, even if the tiles get moved around.

9 Position the tiles in the first column so that they are exactly where you want them to be in relation to each other. Then, using the very tip of the X-ACTO knife, lightly mark the spot on each tile where each jump ring should be attached, as shown here.

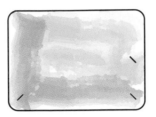

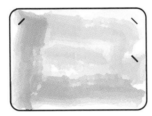

Step 9: Mark where each jump ring should be attached in the first column of tiles.

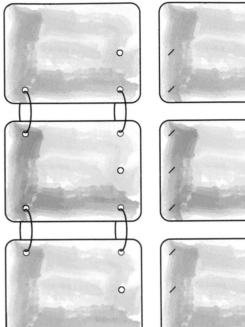

Steps 11–15: Use jump rings to join the tiles in the first column.

Step 16: Mark where each jump ring should be attached in the second column of tiles.

10 Using your drill, bore holes in each tile where you marked them in the preceding step.

11 Using your needle nose pliers, open a jump ring.

Step 11: Open the jump ring.

Tip: To avoid weakening your jump ring, open it by bending the tips of the ring away from each other sideways.

12 Insert the jump ring into the bottom-right hole of the top tile, and then into the top-right hole of the middle tile.

13 Using your needle nose pliers, carefully close the jump ring.

14 Open a jump ring and insert it into the bottom-right hole of the middle tile and then into the top-right hole of the bottom tile.

15 Repeat steps 11–14, this time inserting the jump rings in the holes on the left side of each tile. Your first column is now complete.

16 Repeat steps 9 and 10 on the second column of tiles, marking them as shown.

17 Repeat steps 11–15 to attach the top, middle, and bottom tiles in the second column to each other.

18 Insert a jump ring into the hole on the right side of the tile at the top of the first

column, insert the same jump ring into the hole on the left side of the top tile in the second column, and carefully close the jump ring.

19 Repeat step 18 on the middle 2 tiles in the first and second column.

20 Repeat step 18 on the bottom 2 tiles in the first and second column. You now have 2 complete columns of tiles that have been joined together.

21 Repeat steps 16–20 to attach the remaining columns.

22 After you have added all the columns to the bracelet, it's time to attach the clasp. To begin, position the clasp alongside either end of your bracelet.

23 Using your X-ACTO knife, mark the positions of the clasp's holes on the bracelet's corresponding tiles.

24 Drill the holes in the tiles.

25 Attach the clasp to the end of the bracelet using jump rings.

26 Repeat steps 22–25 to attach the other half of the clasp to the other end of the bracelet. When you position your clasp on the other end of the bracelet, double-check that once the clasp is closed, all of the tiles will line up.

Long Live Vinyl!

Designer: Tiffany Moreland

As the covered wagon lost out to the car, the typewriter made way for the computer, and the telegraph was trumped by the telephone, so, too, was the vinyl record overshadowed by new, better technologies—and with it, the 45 record adapter. For audiophile Luddites everywhere, however, this old-school doodad has remained a potent symbol of their love for vinyl—making it the perfect adornment for the music lover in your life.

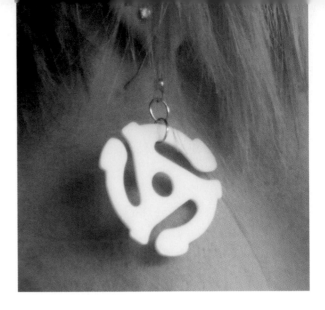

MATERIALS:

- 2 45-record adapters
- 2 fish hook ear wires
- 2 jump rings
- needle nose pliers
- 1 large safety pin
- candle
- matches

Instructions

1 Using the pliers, straighten the safety pin.

Step 1: Straighten the safety pin.

2 Light the candle.

3 Holding the safety pin by its head, hover the sharp end above the flame for a few seconds.

4 Pierce either of the record adapters with the hot safety pin, close to the edge, so that it makes a hole all the way through the plastic. Then remove the safety pin.

5 Repeat step 4 on the other record adapter.

6 Using your pliers, open a jump ring.

Tip: To avoid weakening your jump ring, open it by bending the tips of the ring away from each other sideways.

7 Insert the open jump ring through the hole you created in either record adapter.

8 Feed the jump ring through the hole at the bottom of the ear wire.

Step 6: Opening the jump ring.

9 Using your pliers, close the jump ring by bending the tips back toward each other.

10 Repeat steps 6–9 to assemble the second earring.

Poker Face

Designer: Kate Shoup

You managed to escape Vegas with a single chip still in your pocket, which begs the question, what the heck should you do with it? Rather than relegating it to your junk drawer, try converting it into some bling.

MATERIALS:

- Poker chip

- Drill

- Beading wire (We used Beadalon, the 49-strand variety, 9/10 in. diameter.)

- Cutters (Fine scissors will work, or else a wire cutter.)

- Beads (This is a great opportunity to recycle beads from pieces you're no longer wild about.)

- Clasp

- 2 crimp beads

- Needle nose pliers

- Crimping pliers (These are special pliers available at bead shops. If you don't feel like investing in them, your plain old needle nose pliers will work, although the crimp won't be as solid.)

Instructions

1. Drill a hole near the top of the poker chip.

2. Cut a 24-in. (or thereabouts) length of beading wire.

3. Feed the beading wire through the hole such that the poker chip is at the center point of the wire.

4. Gather both ends of the beading wire together and feed them both through a bead.

5. Add beads to the right half of the beading wire, stopping when you're about 1 or 2 in. from the end.

6. Add a crimp bead to the right half of the wire.

7. Feed the right end of the wire through the loop on your clasp, back through the crimp bead, and through the last bead or two that you added. Tug the excess beading wire with your needle nose pliers to tighten the loop created with the wire—the goal being to have as little space as possible between the last bead of your piece and the crimp bead, and to have just enough space between the crimp bead and the clasp so that the clasp has a bit of wiggle room.

Step 4: Feed both ends of the wire through a bead.

Note: This can take some practice, so don't lose your enthusiasm if it doesn't work quite right on your first try.

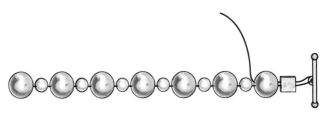

Step 7: Add the clasp to the right end of the beading wire.

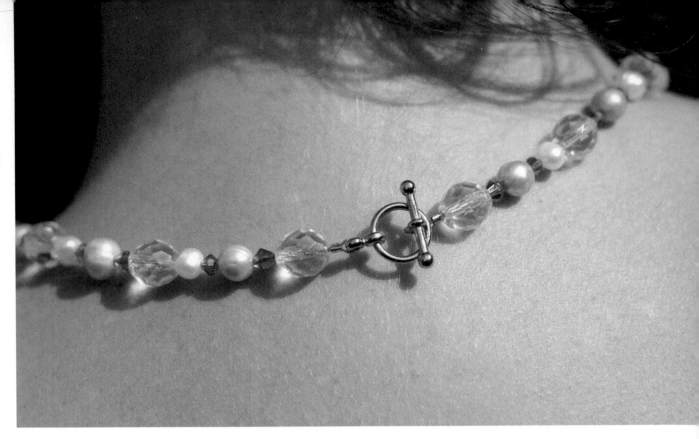

8 Use your pliers to squish the crimp bead.

9 Use your cutters to snip the excess wire from the right side of the piece.

10 Repeat steps 5–9 to complete the left side of the necklace.

Bring Out the Crimp

Using crimping pliers is a bit different from using regular pliers. It's a two-step process. First, place the crimp bead in the crimping pliers' inner jaw—where its "molars" are, if you'll excuse the anthropomorphism—and squeeze to fold the crimp bead in half. Then place the crimp bead *on its side* in the tool's "incisors" and squeeze.

Go Postal

Designer: Andrea Glick-Zenith

Philatelists rejoice! You now have a new outlet for your beloved stamps, be they vintage or new, cancelled or clean: this fantastic brooch. If your stamp collection is a bit lean, consider rifling through the rubbish bins at your local P.O. to see what nifty bits of postage have been tossed.

MATERIALS:

- 1 stamp (This can be vintage or new or perhaps recycled from a letter or package.)
- 1 clear glass cabochon or pebble (These can be found just about anywhere, including arts and craft stores, faux-flower shops, etc.)
- All-in-one glue/sealer/finisher (We used Mod Podge.)
- Water-based polyurethane sealer or nontoxic sealant (We used a polycrylic protective finish made by MINWAX.)
- Nail polish remover
- Old towel (Paper towels will also work.)
- 1 small foam paintbrush
- 1 medium craft paintbrush
- Glue (We like E-6000.)
- 1 3 x 3-in. piece cardstock (This can be recycled or new, white or colored.)
- Scissors (These should be good and sharp.)
- Pin back
- 1 sheet newspaper

Instructions

1. Wipe the flat side of your cabochon with an old towel.

2. Using a foam paintbrush, smear some Mod Podge on the flat side of the cabochon.

   Note: Don't be stingy here; apply liberally.

3. Position the recycled stamp facedown on the flat side of the cabochon and use your fingers to press it into place.

4. Again using your foam paintbrush, apply Mod Podge to the back of the stamp and to any exposed cabochon.

5. Lay a piece of cardstock on your work surface and then place the cabochon flat-side/sticky-side down on the cardstock. Press firmly; you might even place a heavy book or cutting board on top of the cabochon.

6. After allowing sufficient time for the Mod Podge to dry (30 minutes to an hour should do the trick), cut the cardstock away from the cabochon, as close to the edges as you can.

7. Unfold your sheet of newspaper and place the cabochon on it round-side down.

8. Using a craft paintbrush, apply polyurethane sealer to the flat side of the cabochon. Brush the sealer in one direction, taking care to coat all the edges. Allow the sealer to dry. (Again, 30 minutes to an hour should be adequate.)

9. Repeat step 8, this time brushing the sealer in the opposite direction.

10 Remove the cabochon from the news-paper. (This may involve some prying, as the sealer likes to run off the edges of the cabochon.)

11 Pour some nail polish remover onto the old towel. Then, hold the towel in your hand remover up, place the cabochon on it round-side down, and rub like crazy to remove the excess polyurethane, Mod Podge, and newspaper.

12 Find a clean spot on the towel and dry-polish the top of the cabochon.

13 Squeeze the tube of E-6000 glue until a nice glop of adhesive oozes out of the top, and then run the back of the pin back across the glop.

14 Press the pin back onto the flat side of the cabochon, and let it dry overnight.

Note: Even though you applied a sealant, you should probably avoid wearing this pin to, say, Niagara Falls or during monsoon season. It is made of recycled paper, after all.

Vanity Plate

Designer: Allison Strine

Just because your license plate expired doesn't mean it belongs in the trash. Instead, cut it into pieces and solder them into pendants. You may still get pulled over—but it'll be to receive compliments, not tickets.

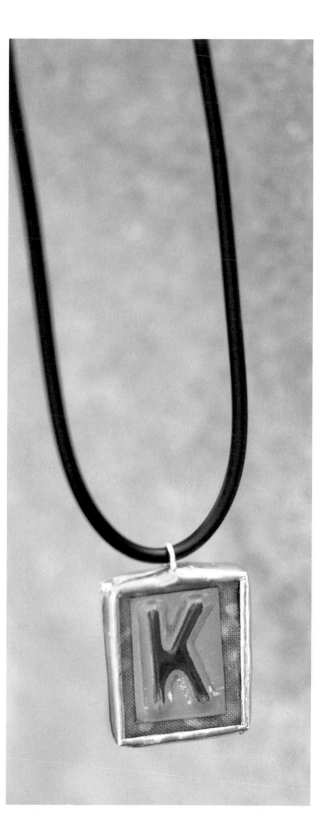

MATERIALS:

- 1 license plate

- Heavy-duty metal shears

- 2 glass rectangles, standard picture-framing thickness (These rectangles should be slightly larger than the portion you plan to cut from the license plate. For example, we cut out a ¾ x 1-in. piece from our plate, so cut our glass rectangles to about 1 x 1¼ in. You can either have these precut or cut them yourself using a glass cutter.)

- Scrap of fabric or paper that's the same size as the glass rectangles

- ⅜-in. wide copper tape (You can obtain this from a stained-glass supplier.)

- Scissors (Opt for ones that aren't your favorites.)

- Solder (Go for the thinner stuff—think 1-2mm.)

- Flux

- Small paintbrush

- Soldering iron

- Burnish tool

- Needle nose pliers

- 1 jump ring (This should be copper, stainless steel, or sterling silver—any material that can be soldered.)

NOTE: Rather than using the size of your license-plate piece to determine how large your glass bits should be, you might need to do the reverse—that is, find some precut glass and use it to determine what size your license plate piece should be. Another option is to recycle microscope slides—although they're pretty fragile, and may contain vestiges of, say, bird-flu (or similar) cells.

Instructions

1 Using your heavy-duty metal shears, cut a small square from the license plate. (We opted for a letter.)

2 Create a "sandwich" by laying 1 of the pieces of glass on your work surface, laying your scrap of fabric or paper on top of the glass facedown, centering the license-plate piece faceup on top of the fabric or paper, and laying the second piece of glass on top of the license-plate piece.

3 Using your scissors, cut a length of copper tape that equals the perimeter of your glass rectangles. (In our case, the length of tape was 4½ in.)

4 Peel the paper backing from the copper tape and lay it vertically, sticky-side up, on your work surface.

5 Lay the left edge of the sandwich faceup on the right portion of the tape.

6 Fold the tape up against the sandwich layers and over the top glass piece.

Step 5: Lay the sandwich on the tape.

Step 6: Fold the tape to secure the left edge of the sandwich.

7 Carefully work the tape around the corner of the sandwich to secure the bottom edge, folding the corners as neatly as possible.

8 Repeat step 7 on the right and top edges of the sandwich.

9 Burnish the tape well on all 4 sides.

Note: *Burnish* is just a fancy way of saying "rub the copper foil to make it as smooth and even as humanly possible."

10 Brush a thin layer of flux all over the copper tape.

11 Solder the tape. To do so, lay the piece on your work surface. (Be sure to use a metal table or fire brick so you don't torch your workspace by accident.) Next, hold the soldering iron in one hand and the solder in the other and then put the tips of both together on the copper tape. Go all the way around the front of the frame in this manner; then go around the back and the sides.

12 Affix the jump ring. To begin, put some solder on the tip of the iron. Then, holding the jump ring with needle nose pliers, position the ring at the center point of the top edge of the sandwich. Apply the soldering iron and push the jump ring into place, holding it steady until it cools.

Put a Cork in It

Designer: Kate Shoup

A night of wine-fueled debauchery can result in more than just tears and recriminations—it can yield this fantastic bracelet that incorporates the corks from your bottles.

MATERIALS:

- 2 corks (For best results, extract the corks from the bottles using a lever- or pump-style wine opener instead of a traditional corkscrew; that way, the corks emerge essentially intact.)

- 24-in. 18-gauge wire (We used copper.)

- X-ACTO knife

- Sturdy needle or bead reamer

- Wire cutters

- Needle nose pliers

- Round nose pliers

- Toggle clasp (Again, ours is copper, to match the wire.)

- 6 beads (Your numbers may vary depending on how large your beads are. Just make sure the beads' holes are wide enough to accommodate the copper wire.)

Instructions

1. Use the X-ACTO knife to carefully cut both corks into thirds. (Do this *after* you have sobered up!)

2. Use the needle or bead reamer to poke a hole through the middle of each cork piece.

3. Using your wire cutters, cut 8 3-in. lengths of copper wire.

4. Form a wrapped loop on the bottom end of 1 3-in. length of wire. To begin, use your needle nose pliers to form a right angle about ¾ in. from the end of the wire, creating an upside-down L or bent-elbow shape.

5. Position the tip of your round nose pliers in the crook of the "elbow" you created.

6. Using your fingers, curl the wire around the round nose pliers to create a loop. When you're finished, the tail of the wire should form a right angle with the stem of the wire.

Step 6: The tail of the wire should form a right angle.

7. Remove the round nose pliers from the inside loop and, holding them with your non-dominant hand, use them to

34

Rubbish!

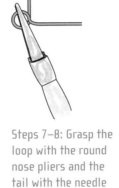

grasp the loop. The wire should be positioned such that the tail portion is pointing upward and passes behind the stem.

8 Place the needle nose pliers in your dominant hand and use them to grasp the tail of the wire.

9 Pull the tail toward you, around the stem, and back to its original position.

Steps 7–8: Grasp the loop with the round nose pliers and the tail with the needle nose pliers.

10 Repeat step 9 a few more times, wrapping the tail around the stem.

11 Use your wire cutters to trim any excess wire from the tail, leaving the stem intact.

12 To ensure that the sharp edge of the wire you just cut doesn't pierce the wrist vein of the person wearing your bracelet, causing her to bleed profusely, use your needle nose pliers to flatten any protruding wire.

Tip: If this wrapped-loop technique is giving you fits, you can opt for a simple loop. To do so, follow steps 4–6 and then simply use your wire cutters to trim the excess wire instead of wrapping it around the stem.

13 Repeat steps 4–12 on the bottom ends of 5 more pieces of 3-in. wire.

14 Repeat steps 4–12 on the bottom end of 1 more piece of wire, but this time, between steps 6 and 7, slip the wire through the loop on either piece of the toggle clasp.

15 Repeat step 14 on the remaining piece of the toggle clasp. Each of the 8 lengths of wire should now feature a wrapped loop at the bottom, with 2 of the 8 attached to pieces of your clasp.

16 Poke a length of wire (opt for one that is not attached to the clasp) through the hole bored into a piece of cork.

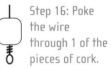

Step 16: Poke the wire through 1 of the pieces of cork.

17 Repeat step 16 with the remaining 5 pieces of cork.

18 Feed half of your beads onto 1 of the lengths of wire that is attached to a piece of the clasp.

19 Repeat steps 4–12 on the top portion of the wire to which you just added beads, this time slipping the wire through the loop at the bottom of 1 of the corked wires between steps 6 and 7.

Step 19: Connect a corked wire to the beaded wire.

21 Connect the remaining lengths of corked wire to the bracelet in the same manner, creating loops from the top part of each connected piece and slipping the wire through the loop at the bottom of the next piece before wrapping the wire.

22 Feed the remaining half of your beads onto the other length of wire that is attached to the clasp.

23 Repeat step 19 to connect the beaded wire and clasp to the rest of the bracelet.

Vive La Resistor

Designer: Mike Mossey

Used to regulate the flow of electrical current in a circuit, resistors are stylishly striped—making them ideal for upcycling. Here you learn to fashion some nifty dangling earrings from resistors, although there's nothing to stop you from attaching resistors to a chain to create a necklace that's, er, irresistible.

MATERIALS:

- 8 electronic resistors   - Wire cutters
- 2 jump rings   - Needle nose pliers
- 2 fishhook ear wires   - Round nose pliers

Instructions

1 Using your wire cutters, trim 1 wire leg off the first resistor, leaving the second wire leg in place.

2 Situate the tip of your needle nose pliers about ½ in. from the tip of the remaining wire leg, grasp the wire with the pliers, and use your fingers to form the wire into a 90-degree angle.

Step 2: Bend the wire at a 90-degree angle.

3 Position the tip of your round nose pliers in the crook of the "elbow" you created in step 2.

4 Using your fingers, curl the wire around the round nose pliers to create a loop. If you didn't quite manage to create a precise circle, use your needle nose pliers to grasp the very tip of the loop and bend the wire so that the tip abuts the stem.

Step 4: Form the wire into a loop.

Note: If necessary, use your wire cutters to trim any excess wire from the tip.

5 Repeat steps 1–4 with the remaining resistors.

6 Using your needle nose pliers, open a jump ring.

Step 6: Open the jump ring.

Tip: To avoid weakening your jump ring, open it by bending the tips of the ring away from each other sideways.

7 Feed 4 of the resistors onto the jump ring.

8 Feed the jump ring through the hole at the bottom of the ear wire.

9 Using your pliers, close the jump ring by bending the tips back toward each other.

10 Repeat steps 6–9 to assemble the second earring.

I'm All Verclamped

Designer: Yvonne Hoyer

You polished off that loaf of bread, and reused the bag in which it was packaged to, say, clean up after your dog. But what about that pesky clamp that sealed the bag? Don't toss it out! Instead, turn it into a nifty charm. You can fasten it to a necklace, bracelet, or, as shown here, earrings. Your clever thriftiness is sure to leave 'em speechless.

MATERIALS:

- 1 bread clamp (i.e., the doodad you use to clamp shut the bag containing your bread)
- Miscellaneous old beads
- 3-in. semi-sturdy wire
- 2 fishhook ear wires
- Scissors
- Drill (A small, nonelectrical one will do.)
- Wire cutter
- Round nose pliers
- Needle nose pliers

Instructions

1 Using your scissors, cut the bread clamp in half longways.

2 Drill a small hole at the top of each piece of the clamp.

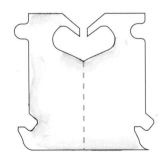

Step 1: Cut the clamp.

Note: If you don't have a drill handy, try the old candle-and-safety-pin trick. Light the candle, hover the pointy end of the pin over the flame until it's nice and hot, and then poke the clamp with the pin to form a hole.

3 Using your wire cutters, cut the 3-in. length of wire into 2 1½-in. pieces.

4 Situate the tip of your needle nose pliers about ½ in. from the tip of 1 piece of wire, grasp the wire with the pliers, and use your fingers to form the wire into a 90-degree angle.

5 Position the tip of your round nose pliers in the crook of the "elbow" you created in step 4.

6 Using your fingers, curl the wire around the round nose pliers to create a loop.

7 If you didn't quite manage to create a precise circle, use your needle nose pliers to grasp the very tip of the loop and bend the wire such that the tip abuts the stem.

Note: If necessary, use your wire cutters to trim any excess wire from the tip.

8 Using your needle nose pliers, open the loop you created in steps 4–7.

9 Slide the wire loop through the hole in either piece of the bread clamp.

10 Use your needle nose pliers to close the loop.

11 Feed a few beads onto the wire, leaving about ½ in. of bare wire at the top.

12 Repeat steps 4–8 to create and open a loop at the top of the wire, above the beads.

13 Feed the open loop at the top of the wire through the loop comprising the bottom of your fishhook ear wire.

14 Use your needle nose pliers to close the loop.

15 Repeat steps 4–14 to assemble the second earring.

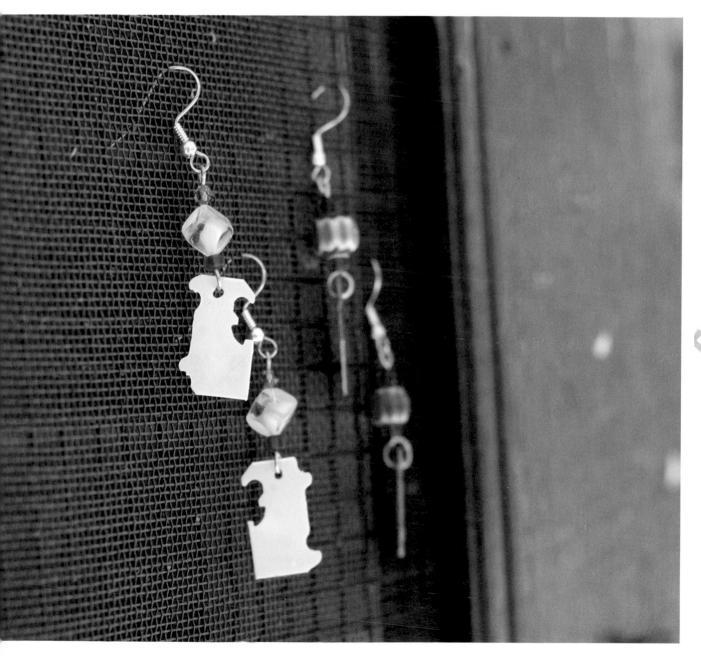

Accessorize, Don't Excess-orize

4

Cuff Daddy

Designer: Tiffany Moreland

So you've chucked your soulless office job to pursue your lifelong dream of launching an eco-friendly garden-gnome store—meaning you have a closet full of workaday-doldrums neckties, but no office to wear them to. To ensure they don't go to waste, try fashioning them into ultracool cuffs.

MATERIALS:

- 1 tie (we opted for vintage.)
- 1 large button
- Sewing machine
- Thread
- Needle
- Seam ripper
- Scissors

Instructions

1 Cut the skinny end of the tie so that it measures approximately 2½ in. longer than your wrist. For example, a person with a wrist that is 7 in. around will need to cut a 9½-in. length of tie.

2 Using your sewing machine, stitch the cut end of the tie closed. (Opt for a tight zigzag stitch here.)

3 Use your sewing machine to stitch a buttonhole on the other end of the cuff. The buttonhole should be as wide as your button.

4 Using your seam ripper, open the buttonhole.

5 Sew the button onto the cuff, about ½ in. from the cut end.

No Dice

Designer: Kate Shoup

Just because you lost the World Series of Dice doesn't mean you should pitch all your dice; instead, upcycle them into fashion accessories. This project shows you how to create nifty embellished bobby pins with leftover dice, but you could just as easily adhere them to barrettes or even bracelets.

MATERIALS:

- 1 die

- 1 bobby pin with pad (Ours has a pad that measures 10mm across.)

- Adhesive (We're fans of E-6000.)

Instructions

1. Place a small amount of adhesive on the bobby pin pad.

2. Press the die firmly onto the pad.

3. Prop up the bobby pin so the die stays in place and let it dry. (Overnight is best.)

Pick of the Litter

Designer: Kate Shoup

Tossing your used guitar picks into a crowd of adoring fans is, frankly, a waste—especially when you can use them to create this nifty key ring. (Note that you can just as easily use the technique outlined here to craft cool-looking earrings or a nifty necklace.)

MATERIALS:

- 9 guitar picks (We chose picks of varying sizes and colors.)

- 9 jump rings

- 1 key ring

- Needle nose pliers

- Large safety pin

- 3-in. length of chain (Make sure the links are large enough to fit onto the key ring.)

- Candle

- Matches

Instructions

1 Using your pliers, straighten the safety pin.

Step 1: Straighten the safety pin.

2 Light the candle.

3 Holding the safety pin by its head, hover the sharp end above the flame for a few seconds.

4 Pierce 1 of the guitar picks with the hot safety pin, close to the edge of the pick's pointy end, so that it makes a hole all the way through the plastic. Then remove the safety pin.

5 Repeat steps 3–4 on the remaining 8 picks.

Step 6: Open the jump ring.

6 Using your pliers, open a jump ring.

Tip: To avoid weakening your jump ring, open it by bending the tips of the ring away from each other sideways.

7 After determining the order in which you want the picks to be arranged on the chain, insert the open jump ring through the hole you created in 1 of the picks.

8 Feed the jump ring through the link at the end of the chain.

9 Using your pliers, close the jump ring by bending the tips back toward each other.

10 Repeat steps 6–9 to add the remaining picks to the chain, moving up a few links each time.

Note: The number of links separating each pick will vary depending on how large your links are. We added a pick to every other link.

11 Attach the key ring to the topmost link.

Cover Me

Designer: Kate Shoup

Sure, iPods are cool . . . so cool, in fact, that practically everybody has one. So how can you set yours apart? By constructing this nifty holder—made out of an old album cover, no less. We're not gonna lie to you: This project involves some sweat equity. But trust us: It's worth it. (Note that this iPod cover is designed for the classic video iPod that features a click wheel; if you use a different type of iPod, you'll want to measure it to determine the correct size for the holder and the correct placement of any necessary openings.)

MATERIALS:

- 1 record album cover
- Sturdy X-ACTO knife
- Ruler
- Poker chip (or other 1½-in.(ish) disc)
- Marking pen
- Sharp pencil
- Hole punch
- Glue gun and glue sticks

- 1 15 x 8-in. piece transparent contact paper
- Scissors
- Touch fasteners (We suggest velcro brand; get the kind with adhesive on the back.)
- 1mm ribbon

Instructions

Cut Out the Holder

1 Lay the album cover facedown on your work surface.

2 Using your ruler and marking pen, measure and mark on the backside of the album cover as shown here. (Be sure the area you mark on the back corresponds to the area on the front of the album cover you want featured on your iPod holder.)

3 Using your ruler as a straightedge, cut out the shape you marked with the X-ACTO knife.

Note: Because of the thickness of the cover, you'll likely need to make several passes with the knife for each cut.

Score the Holder

4 Using your ruler and pencil, carefully mark the front side of the album cover as shown here. These marks will serve as guidelines for scoring the holder, which you must do in order to fold it into shape.

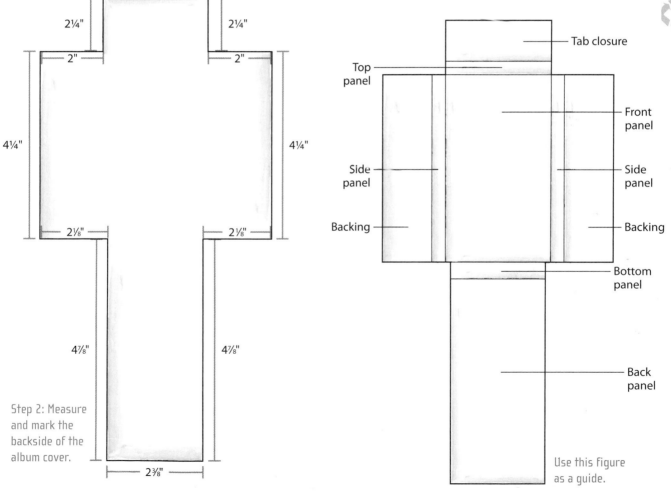

Step 2: Measure and mark the backside of the album cover.

Use this figure as a guide.

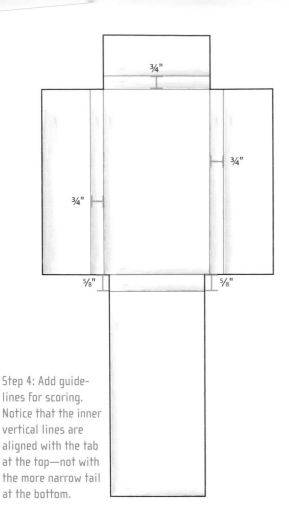

Step 4: Add guidelines for scoring. Notice that the inner vertical lines are aligned with the tab at the top—not with the more narrow tail at the bottom.

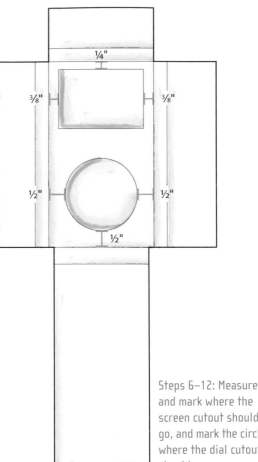

Steps 6–12: Measure and mark where the screen cutout should go, and mark the circle where the dial cutout should go.

5 Using your ruler as a straightedge, gently score the guidelines you drew in step 4 on the front side of the album cover with the X-ACTO knife. When you are finished scoring, you should be able to easily fold the album cover along the guidelines (but leave them unfolded for the time being).

Cut Out Openings

6 Your next step is to cut out an opening for the screen. To begin, use your ruler and pencil to carefully mark a 2 × 1½-in. rectangle on the front panel. Position it such that the top line of the rectangle is ¼ in. from the top of the panel, and the sides of the rectangle are ⅜ in. from the sides of the panel.

7 Using your ruler as a straightedge, cut out the rectangle with the X-ACTO knife.

8 Next, cut out an opening for the dial. To begin, locate the center point of the line comprising the bottom of the front panel and then measure up ½ in., lightly marking the spot with your pencil.

9 Measure up 1¼ in. along the right side of the front panel and then measure in ½ in., lightly marking the spot with your pencil.

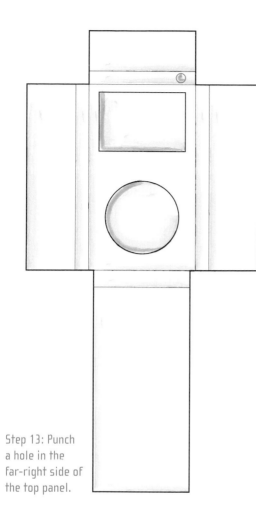

Step 13: Punch a hole in the far-right side of the top panel.

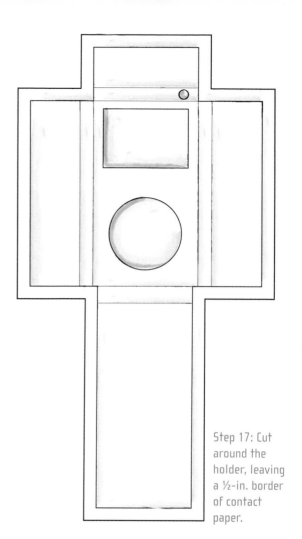

Step 17: Cut around the holder, leaving a ½-in. border of contact paper.

10 Measure up 1¼ in. along the left side of the front panel and then measure in ½ in., lightly marking the spot with your pencil.

11 Lay the poker chip on the front panel, placing it according to the marks you made in steps 8–10. Then, using your pencil, lightly trace around the chip.

12 Using your X-ACTO knife, cut out the circle.

Note: One approach is to use the poker chip as a guide as you cut. Alternatively, start by slicing up the circle much as you would a pizza and then cut around the "crust."

13 Use your hole punch to punch a hole on the far right side of the top panel. This will allow you to insert your headphones in the iPod's headphone jack when it's in the holder.

Laminate the Holder

14 Using your scissors, cut a piece of transparent contact paper that is roughly 15 × 8 in.

15 Peel the backing from the contact paper and place the contact paper on your work surface sticky-side-up.

Rubbish!

16 Lay the iPod holder on the contact paper facedown, centering it as best you can. Press firmly for a good seal.

Note: If you wind up with wrinkles or bubbles, gently peel the contact paper from the iPod holder and re-adhere it.

17 Using your scissors, cut around the holder, leaving a border of contact paper that's about ½-in. wide.

18 Use your marking pen to draw a line on the contact paper that starts at the top-left corner of the tab closure and travels up and to the right at a 45-degree angle.

19 Draw another line on the contact paper that starts at the top-left corner of the closure, this time traveling down and to the left at a 45-degree angle.

20 Using your scissors, cut along the lines you drew in steps 18 and 19.

21 Repeat steps 18–20 to "triangle off" the remaining corners of the piece.

22 Make 4 more cuts to the contact paper, as shown here.

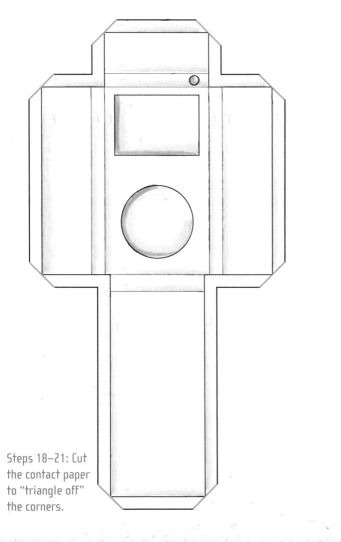

Steps 18–21: Cut the contact paper to "triangle off" the corners.

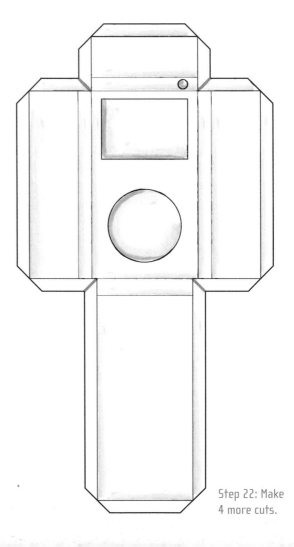

Step 22: Make 4 more cuts.

23 Pull the flap of contact paper that runs along the top of the tab closure over the top edge of the iPod holder and fold it over, pressing it firmly onto the backside of the holder.

24 Repeat step 23 on the remaining contact paper flaps.

25 Using your X-ACTO knife, cut the contact paper that covers the rectangular opening. Start in the top-left corner of the rectangle and cut diagonally to the bottom-right corner.

26 Repeat step 25, starting in the top-right corner and cutting diagonally to the bottom-left corner. Notice that you now have 4 triangular flaps of contact paper.

27 Pull the top triangular flap up and over the edge of the rectangle, fold it over, and press it firmly onto the backside of the holder.

28 Repeat step 27 with the remaining 3 triangular flaps.

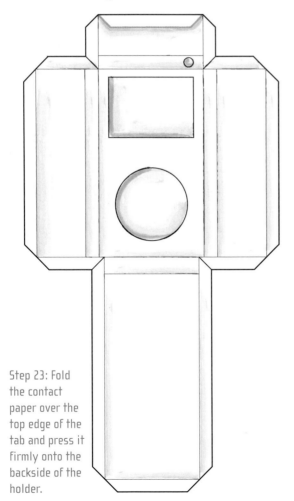

Step 23: Fold the contact paper over the top edge of the tab and press it firmly onto the backside of the holder.

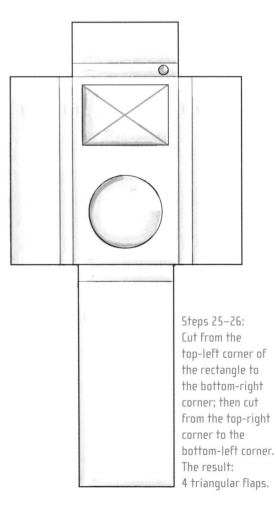

Steps 25–26: Cut from the top-left corner of the rectangle to the bottom-right corner; then cut from the top-right corner to the bottom-left corner. The result: 4 triangular flaps.

29 Using your X-ACTO knife, cut the contact paper covering the circle on the front panel pizza style, but this time leave the "crust" intact. The result is several thin triangular "slices."

30 Pull any 1 of the slices over the edge of the circle, fold it over, and press it firmly onto the backside of the holder.

31 Repeat step 30 with the remaining "slices."

32 Using your hole punch, punch out the contact paper covering the hole on the far-right side of the top panel.

Assemble the Holder

33 Fold the holder so the top of the back panel lines up with the top of the front panel.

34 Use your glue gun to squeeze hot glue on the backside of the pieces of backing.

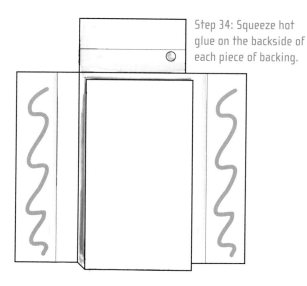

Step 34: Squeeze hot glue on the backside of each piece of backing.

35 Fold the side panels around and firmly press the pieces of backing against the back panel, holding them in place until the glue dries.

36 Cut a 1-in. square piece of Velcro.

37 Adhere the rough half of the Velcro on the backside of the tab closure.

38 Line up the closure with the back of the holder to determine where the fuzzy half of the Velcro should go and adhere it accordingly.

39 Using your scissors, cut an 8-in. length of ribbon.

40 Squeeze a dot of hot glue on the inside of the left side panel, about 1 in. from the top.

41 Firmly press 1 end of the ribbon onto the dot of hot glue.

42 Repeat steps 40–41 on the other side panel to attach the other end of the ribbon.

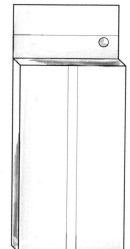

Step 35: Fold the side panels.

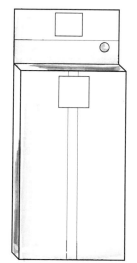

Steps 37–38: Adhere the Velcro.

Check It

Designers: Heather MacFarlane and Mark Kirk

If you recently finished painting your home, rest assured that you don't have to throw that tarp away. It can easily be upcycled into bags, wallets, and, as featured here, checkbook covers.

MATERIALS:

- Tarp

- Shears

- Sewing machine

- Thread (We opted for orange thread, for contrast.)

- Invisible tape (such as Scotch brand)

Instructions

1 Cut a 7⅛ × 6¾-in. rectangle from the tarp.

2 Cut a 6¾ × 3-in. rectangle from the tarp.

3 Repeat step 2, cutting a second 6¾ × 3-in. rectangle.

4 Lay the 7⅛ × 6¾-in. rectangle facedown on your work surface, with the 6¾-in. edges comprising the top and bottom of the rectangle.

5 Lay 1 of the 6¾ × 3-in. rectangles along the bottom of the larger rectangle.

6 Tape the top edge of the 6¾ × 3-in. rectangle to the larger rectangle to help keep it in place while you sew.

7 Lay the remaining 6¾ × 3-in. rectangle along the top of the larger rectangle.

8 Tape the bottom edge of this 6¾ × 3-in. rectangle to the larger rectangle to keep it in place.

9 Sew all the way around the large rectangle using a straight stitch, leaving a ¼-in. seam allowance. Go slowly, taking care to keep the edges of the smaller rectangles aligned with the larger ones.

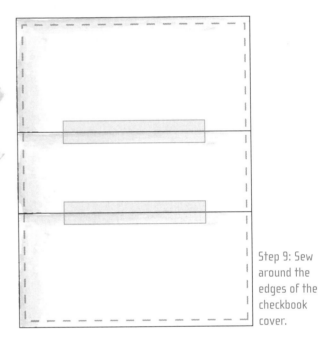

Step 9: Sew around the edges of the checkbook cover.

10 Carefully peel the tape from the tarp.

11 Fold the checkbook cover in half widthwise, pressing firmly along the fold to make it permanent.

As the Wool Turns

Designers: Allison Brideau and Melissa Mazgaj

You're at a thrift store/garage sale/ Dumpster, and you spot a quality wool turtleneck sweater, ripe for the plucking. The dilemma: Your closet is already stuffed with similar garments. What to do? Pluck away and refashion the sweater into a nifty purse.

MATERIALS:

- Wool turtleneck sweater (Ours is a ladies' XL.)

- Washing machine and dryer

- Measuring tape

- Pins

- Shears

- Embroidery scissors

- Sewing machine

- Sewing thread (Try to match up the color with the sweater.)

- Tapestry yarn (Ours was off-white.)

- Sewing needle

- Embroidery needle

- 1 scarf

- 1 button

NOTE: Although our sweater was 100 percent wool, wool blends are also acceptable as long as the sweater is at least 80 percent wool.

Instructions

1 Wash the wool sweater in the washing machine using hot water.

2 Dry the sweater in the dryer. This pulls the fibers of the sweater together, shrinking it. (Trust us: You haven't lived until you've shrunk a sweater.)

3 Lay the munchkin-sized sweater on your work surface and, starting at the seam under either arm, use your measuring tape to measure inward 5 in., roughly even with the neck of the sweater. Mark the measurement with a pin.

Note: If your sweater is a different size from ours, then the 5-in. measurement may not apply; just insert the pin so it lines up roughly with the neck of the sweater.

4 Repeat step 3, starting the measurement under the other arm.

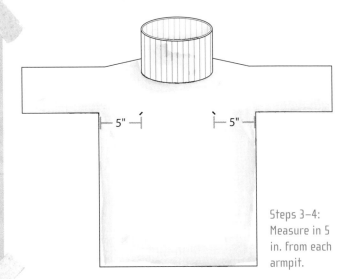

Steps 3–4: Measure in 5 in. from each armpit.

5 Using your shears, cut inward from the left underarm seam to the pin you inserted.

6 Repeat step 5, starting at the other underarm seam.

7 Next, cut upward toward the neck, and then around the neck, cutting along the seam where the neck meets the body of the sweater.

8 Starting about halfway between the neck and the pins, cut across the sweater to create the purse's front flap.

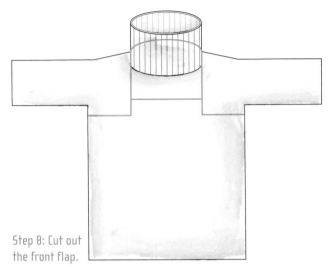

Step 8: Cut out the front flap.

9 Trim any uneven material to tidy things up.

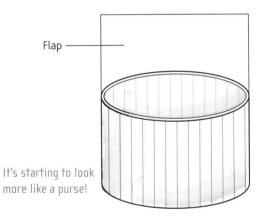

Flap

It's starting to look more like a purse!

10 Using a straight stitch, sew a ¼-in. seam across the bottom of the purse—i.e., the end opposite the one with the flap. (Note that the purse is right-side-out here.)

11 Using your sewing needle and thread, stitch 1 end of your scarf to the side of the purse.

12 Repeat step 11, stitching the other end of the scarf to the other side of the purse.

13 Using your measuring tape, locate the center of the front of the purse, and then use your needle and thread to affix the button there.

14 After determining where on the flap the buttonhole for the button you affixed in step 13 belongs, use your shears to cut a small slit in the flap.

15 Thread your embroidery needle with your off-white tapestry yarn and, using a blanket stitch, reinforce the buttonhole.

The Blanket Stitch (Not to Be Confused with Michael Jackson's Kid)

Working a blanket stitch results in a series of backward L-shapes, making it perfect for reinforcing a buttonhole or any other type of raw edge. When working the stitch, envision two imaginary lines. The first, which we'll call "line A," is where the base of each L shape will appear. (In our case, line A equals the raw edge of the buttonhole.) The other, which we'll call "line B," runs parallel to line A and represents the height of the stem of each L shape.

To begin, start your thread on the left side of line A, draw the thread diagonally up and to the right, and then pass your needle through line B from front to back. Rather than pull the thread all the way through, however, leave a loop in place. Then, on line A, directly beneath the hole through which the needle passed in line B, draw your needle and thread through your fabric from back to front, and then pass the needle and thread through the loop you created. Pull tight to secure it; this completes the stem portion of the "L" shape. Repeat to work the next stitch.

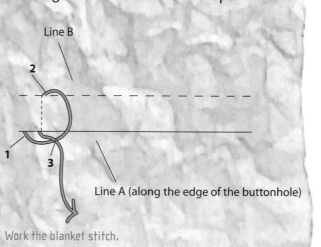

Work the blanket stitch.

Clutch Player

Designer: April Alden

Do you miss those bygone days of folding aluminum lawn chairs—the kind with festive woven webbing? If so, then this project is for you. It repurposes the colorful webbing into a gorgeous clutch that's durable, light-weight, and positively screams summer.

MATERIALS:

- 1 44-in. length of lawn chair webbing (Ours was roughly 3 in. wide.)

- 1 70-in. length of lawn chair webbing (Ours was roughly 1¾ in. wide and in a contrasting color.)

- 1 9-in. zipper

- Clear plastic thread

- 1 20-in. length strap webbing for handle

- Bias tape (Scraps of material will also work.)

- Measuring tape

- Sewing machine

- Zipper foot for sewing machine

- Scissors

- Pins

- Iron (A lighter will also work.)

NOTE: If either piece of your lawn chair webbing is of a different width than the pieces cited here, it will affect how long the second piece of webbing should be. For example, suppose your first length of webbing is 3½ in. wide instead of 3 in. and that the second length is 3 in. wide. To determine how long the second piece of webbing should be: Multiply the width of the first length of webbing by 4 and add 2 to the result (so, in this case, [3½ x 4] + 2 = 16). Then divide the length of the zipper by the width of the second piece of webbing (9 ÷ 3 = 3). Finally, multiply the result of the first calculation by the result of the second calculation (in this example, 16 x 3 = 48).

Instructions

1 Use your scissors to cut the 44-in. length of webbing (we'll call this "first-color webbing") into 4 pieces of equal length, each one 11 in. long.

2 Use your scissors to cut the 70-in. length of webbing (we'll call this "second-color webbing") into 5 pieces of equal length, each one 14 in. long.

Note: Step 2 assumes that your webbing is the same width as ours. If it isn't, divide the length of your zipper by the width of your second-color webbing to determine how many pieces you need. So, for example, using the scenario mentioned previously, where the zipper is 9 in. long and the second-color webbing was 3 in. wide (and 48 in. long), you'd cut it into 3 pieces, each one 16-in. long

3 Heat-treat the cut edges of each length of lawn chair webbing and the cut edges of the strap webbing to prevent fraying. One method is to hold the end up to a hot iron for a few seconds; alternatively, singe the edges with a lighter.

Note: Unless you want to become a sad statistic, be careful with this heat-treating step; the fumes can be toxic. If you can, perform this step outside or use a respirator with cartridges for fumes. Do not perform this step in the room where you are planning on working; the fumes will linger.

4 Lay the 5 lengths of second-color webbing on your work surface, lining them up vertically.

5 Starting about ½ in. in from the top (this is so you'll have room to fold the edges over later), weave 1 length of first-color webbing horizontally in an under/over fashion through the lengths of second-color webbing, pinning it into place.

6 Use your sewing machine to sew all 4 sides of the woven webbing.

Step 7: Weave the remaining lengths of first-color webbing through second-color webbing.

8 Check your solid woven sheet for loose string, snipping any bits you find.

9 Fold down the ½ in. of webbing you left in step 5, pin it, and sew it into place.

10 Repeat step 9 on the webbing on the opposite end.

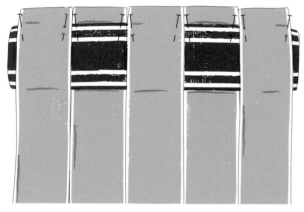

Steps 5–6: Weave a length of first-color webbing through the lengths of second-color webbing, pin it, and then sew all 4 sides of the woven webbing to keep it in place.

7 Repeat steps 5 and 6 to weave the remaining lengths of first-color webbing, taking care to keep your weave tight and square.

Steps 9–10: Fold over the top and bottom edges of the weave, pin, and sew into place.

11 For a finished look, lay a length of bias tape over the top fold, pin it, and sew it into place.

12 Repeat step 11 on the other fold.

13 Align the fold along the top of the woven sheet with the zipper, pin it, and sew it into place.

14 Turn the bag inside-out and zip it closed.

15 Fold the strap webbing in half lengthwise and sew the 2 ends together.

16 After you decide which side of the bag you want the strap to be on, pin it on the inside of one edge, toward the top, with the ends sticking out, keeping it parallel with the zipper.

Step 16: Pin the strap into place.

17 On the side of the bag with the strap, pin and sew the ends of the bag together starting at the bottom and going toward the zipper. Run a back stitch on the strap to ensure that it is secure. (To strengthen the seam, consider repeating this step a few times.)

Note: Not all sewing machines will be happy about sewing through this many layers, especially over the handle, so don't rush it. Also, you may need to adjust the tension on your machine.

18 Unzip the bag just enough to allow you to get your hand inside the bag in order to unzip it once you sew the other edge.

19 Pin and sew the remaining edge of the bag, starting at the bottom and working toward the zipper.

20 Trim any excess material.

21 Heat-treat the sewn edges, again ensuring you don't asphyxiate yourself or others. Then let the bag cool.

22 Turn the bag right-side-out and stuff it with all the things you cannot live without.

Mag Bag

Designer: Debby Grogan

Okay, I'll admit it: I'm a magazine junkie. An ungodly number of magazines find their way to my mailbox each month— *People, The Economist, O, allure, Real Simple, Vanity Fair, ReadyMade* . . . the list is alarmingly long. This project offers a great way to repurpose some of that content into wearable art.

MATERIALS:

- 1 magazine
- 1 medium-sized piece poster board or some card stock (Some old cereal boxes work perfectly.)
- Glue stick
- 3 pieces scrap paper
- Scissors
- Shears
- 1 yd. medium to heavy clear vinyl
- Ruler
- Fine-point permanent marker (such as a Sharpie) or ballpoint pen
- 1 spool cotton hand-quilting thread
- Sewing machine
- 2 sewing needles that can sew through leather (One is bound to break on your first try.)
- Large sticker (We like the Priority Mail stickers, available for free from the post office.)
- Clear packing tape
- ½ yd. fabric (An old sheet or a really large man's shirt will also do.)
- Iron
- 2 7/16-in. grommets
- Sturdy X-ACTO knife
- Grommet tool
- 2 shower curtain hooks (We like the metal ones that are shaped like light bulbs.)
- 1 dog collar chain

Instructions

Cut the Magazine and Other Paper Pieces

1 Using your scissors, carefully cut the front cover from your magazine and trim it to the desired size. This will be used to decorate the front of your bag.

2 Cut a full page from the magazine's interior (or the magazine's back cover) to serve as the back of your bag. It should be the same size as the page you cut in step 1.

3 Cut 2 pieces of poster board to the same size as the pages you cut in steps 1 and 2.

4 Cut 2 pieces of poster board that are as tall as the pages you cut in steps 1 and 2, but 2½ in. wide.

5 Using the glue stick, adhere the magazine cutouts to the poster board you cut in step 3.

Note: If you like, you can cut magazine pages that are the same size as the poster board you cut in step 4 and adhere them to the cardboard to pep up the sides of the bag.

6 Cut 2 pieces of scrap paper to the same size as the pages you cut in steps 1 and 2.

7 Cut 2 pieces of scrap paper to the same size as the poster board you cut in step 4.

Prepare the Vinyl

8 Fold the 1-yd. piece of vinyl in half, and position the vinyl so that the fold runs horizontally along the top.

9 Using your Sharpie and a ruler, draw a horizontal line all the way across the vinyl that's 1 in. from the fold.

10 Again using your Sharpie and a ruler, draw a vertical line all the way down the vinyl that's 1-in. from the left edge.

11 Still using your Sharpie and a ruler, draw another vertical line that's 3 in. from the line you drew in step 10.

12 Using your ruler, measure the width of the magazine's front cover. For the sake of example, let's say it's 7 in.

13 Draw another vertical line that's 7 in. (or whatever the width of your magazine cover is) from the line you drew in step 11.

14 Draw another vertical line that's 3 in. from the line you drew in step 13.

15 Draw another vertical line that's 7 in. (or whatever the width of your magazine cover is) from the line you drew in step 14.

16 Draw 1 more vertical line that's 1 in. from the line you drew in step 15.

17 Using your shears, cut along the line you drew in step 16. (The vinyl should still be folded in half; you'll want to take care to ensure it doesn't get skewed by making sure the edges remain lined up.)

18 On the remnant vinyl, cut out a rectangle that's 4 in. wide, and as long as the cover is wide plus 2 in. (So, for example, if your magazine cover is 7 in. wide, your rectangle should be 4 in. wide and 9 in. long.) This will serve as the bottom of your bag.

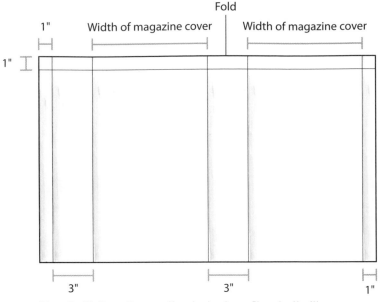

Steps 9–16: Draw lines on the vinyl using a Sharpie. You'll use these lines in lieu of pins when sewing the vinyl to ensure everything lines up correctly.

19 Position the vinyl rectangle you cut in step 18 with the long side along the top.

20 Using your Sharpie and a ruler, draw a horizontal line across the rectangle that's 1 in. from the top.

21 Draw another horizontal line across the rectangle that's 1 in. from the bottom.

22 Draw a vertical line down the side of the rectangle that's 1 in. from the left edge.

23 Draw a vertical line down the side of the rectangle that's 1 in. from the right edge.

Steps 20–23: Map out the bottom of the bag.

Stitch the Vinyl

24 Thread your sewing machine with the hand-quilting thread, also making a bobbin out of the thread.

25 Remove the machine's pressure foot and cover it with the sticker you lifted from the post office.

26 Using a 3-space straight stitch, stitch the large piece of vinyl along the horizontal line you drew in step 9.

Note: Keep good tension on the vinyl to help guide it through the machine. Also, don't try to be all Speedy Gonzales about it; you'll rip the vinyl and/or break the thread if you do. (That said, no matter how careful you are or how slowly you sew, the thread *will* break. Swearing is no help.)

27 Still using a 3-space straight stitch, stitch along the vertical line you drew in step 10.

28 Lay 1 of the 2½-in. wide pieces of scrap paper you cut in step 7 between the 2 layers of vinyl, nestled against the seam you stitched in step 27. This helps keep the layers from sticking together like thighs on a vinyl-covered sofa.

29 Still using a 3-space straight stitch, stitch along the vertical line you drew in step 11.

30 Lay 1 of the pieces of scrap paper you cut in step 6 between the 2 layers of vinyl, nestled against the seam you stitched in step 29.

31 Stitch along the vertical line you drew in step 13.

32 Lay the remaining 2½-in. wide piece of scrap paper you cut in step 7 between the 2 layers of vinyl, nestled against the seam you stitched in step 31.

33 Stitch along the vertical line you drew in step 14.

34 Lay the remaining piece of scrap paper you cut in step 6 between the 2 layers of vinyl, nestled against the seam you stitched in step 33.

35 Stitch along the vertical line you drew in step 15.

Add the Bottom

36 Lay the vinyl rectangle you cut out in step 18 horizontally on the larger piece of vinyl, aligning the lines you drew on the rectangle in steps 20 and 22 with the lines you drew in steps 9 and 11.

37 Starting at the intersecting lines on the left side of the rectangle, stitch the rectangle onto the larger piece of vinyl. Stop stitching when you reach the intersecting lines on the right side of the rectangle.

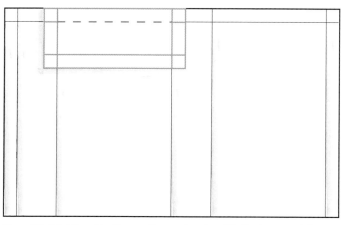

Steps 36–37: Align the line on the rectangle with the top-most line on the larger piece of vinyl along the portion that will contain the magazine cover and stitch as shown.

38 Continue attaching the bottom of the bag onto the body of the bag by matching the vertical line on the right side of the rect-angle with the horizontal line below the fold in the vinyl and stitching from left to right to the next vertical line in the large vinyl panel. (Note that you're sewing the bag inside-out here.)

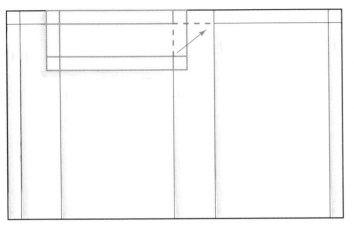

Step 38: Sew the short side of the rectangle to the side panel of the bag.

39 Repeat step 38 on the left side, match-ing the vertical line on the left side of the rectangle with the horizontal line below the fold and stitching from right to left to the next vertical line in the large vinyl panel.

40 Align the left-most line in the vinyl panel (i.e., the one you drew in step 9) with the right-most line (i.e., the one you drew in step 15) and stitch them together.

41 Sew the remaining bottom seam.

Finish the Vinyl

42 Turn the bag right-side-out. (Note that this is easier said than done.)

43 Insert the magazine's front cover between the 2 layers of vinyl that com-prise the front of the purse.

44 Repeat step 43 for the remaining maga-zine cutouts to embellish the back and sides of the purse, removing the scrap paper that you inserted earlier.

45 Cut the excess vinyl from the top of the bag, leaving an allowance of about ½ in.

46 Cut the allowance at each corner of the bag such that you can fold the vinyl over on the inside of the bag.

47 Tape down the folded vinyl with clear packing tape.

48 Cut a piece of poster board that has the same dimensions as the bottom of your bag.

Note: If you like, you can add a magazine cut-out to this piece of poster board to deco-rate the bottom of the bag.

49 Lay the poster board in the bottom of the bag, fold the vinyl seam allowance in the bottom of the bag over the poster board, and tape it into place with your clear packing tape.

Add the Lining

50 The lining for your bag will look similar to a pillowcase. To begin fashioning it, fold your piece of fabric in half, right-side-in, and cut it such that the fold equals the width of the bag's front panel, plus half the width of the bag's side panel, plus a 1-in. seam allowance. For example, in our case, the fold should be 9½ in. wide (i.e., 7 in. for the front panel, 1½ in. for half the side panel, and 1 in. for the seam allowance).

51 Sew up the left side of the "pillowcase."

52 Sew up the right side of the "pillowcase."

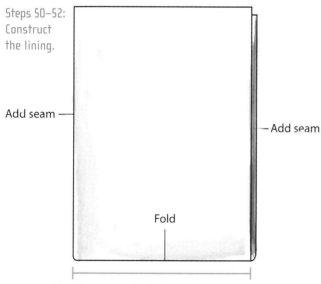

Steps 50–52: Construct the lining.

Add seam —

— Add seam

Fold

Width of front panel + half width of side panel + 1"

53 In the bottom-left corner of the pillowcase, cut out a square whose sides are equal to half the depth of the bag. (For example, if the bag is 3 in. deep, then the square should have sides that are 1½ in. across.)

54 Repeat step 53 in the bottom-right corner of the pillowcase.

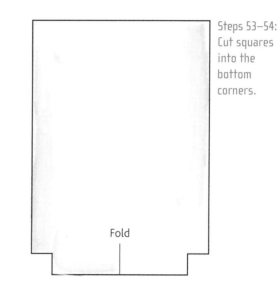

Steps 53–54: Cut squares into the bottom corners.

Fold

55 Pinch the corners of the bottom-left square together to create a triangle shape, and sew around it.

56 Repeat step 55 with the bottom-right square corner.

57 Cut excess fabric from the top of the lining, leaving a couple inches as a seam allowance.

58 Fold the seam allowance over and iron it into place.

59 Turn the lining right-side-out and insert it into the bag.

60 To secure the lining, sew it into place by stitching a seam all the way around the top of the bag.

Step 60:
Sew around
the top of
the bag to
stitch the
lining into
place.

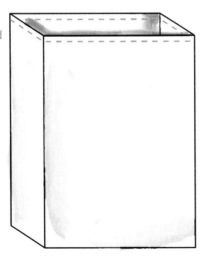

Create the Strap

61 On either side panel, measure down from the top of the bag 1½ in. and use your Sharpie to mark an X that's the size of your grommet.

62 Repeat step 61 on the other side panel.

Step 61:
X marks
the spot
where the
grommets
will go.

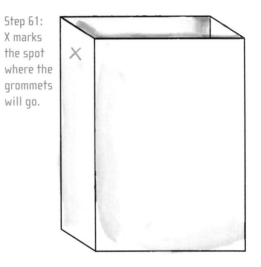

63 Using a sturdy X-ACTO knife, cut along each X through the vinyl.

64 Insert a grommet into either X and install it per the manufacturer's specs.

65 Repeat step 64 on the remaining X.

66 Feed a shower curtain hook through either grommet and attach one end of the dog collar chain.

67 Repeat step 66 with the remaining shower curtain hook.

Note: For added strength and durability, consider soldering the shower curtain hooks closed.

Paper or Plastic?

Designer: Melissa Nappi

It's the eternal dilemma: Paper or plastic? If you opt for paper, you claim responsibility for the demise of a tree. But if you choose plastic, you become culpable in the release of toxic chemicals during the production of the bag. Of course, the simple solution is to bring your own bag, preferably of the nondisposable variety. But if you forget, opt for plastic and then fashion the carriers into this nifty purse.

MATERIALS:

- 3 plastic bags (like the ones you get at the grocery store)
- Iron
- Ironing board
- Wax paper
- Scissors
- Measuring tape

Instructions

Construct the Body of the Bag

1. Cover the portion of your ironing board on which you'll be working with wax paper.

Note: Make it a point to set up your ironing board in a well-ventilated area. Chances are you've already lost plenty of brain cells during your life; now's no time to lose more.

2. Turn the iron on to the medium/synthetic setting and let it heat up.

3. Using your scissors, cut the handles and bottoms from all 3 of your plastic bags and set them aside. (You'll use them later.)

4. Flatten the cut bags and lay them on top of each other. If the bags on the top and/or bottom of the stack feature text or graphics, ensure that the ink side of the bag faces the middle of the stack. What you're doing here is creating layers out of the 3 bags—6 layers in total. When you iron the bags, the layers will fuse, creating a thicker plastic; this makes it harder to rip.

5. Trim the edges of the layers to match up.

6. Fold the layers to create a pocket, leaving about 2 in. along the top for a flap.

7. Cut a sheet of wax paper that's slightly narrower than the interior of the pocket but tall enough to stick out the top and insert it in the pocket. (This is so you don't accidentally fuse the purse closed when you iron it.)

8 Lay a second sheet of wax paper over the top of the folded layers, covering them completely. (This is to prevent the purse from sticking to the iron.)

Note: NEVER PUT THE IRON DIRECTLY ON THE PLASTIC. Sorry—we're not yelling at you. It's just that we really want to emphasize this point. If the hot iron touches the plastic, the plastic will stick to the iron, which will suck.

9 Move the iron all over the wax paper on top of the purse for 5–10 seconds, allowing extra time on the edges and seams.

10 Flip the purse over and, with the wax paper you laid on the ironing board in step 1 stuck to the purse, iron it again for 5–10 seconds.

11 After letting the purse cool for a moment, peel the wax paper off the front and back of the purse.

12 If any portions of the purse failed to fuse properly, run the iron over them a second time, using wax paper as before. (Peel the wax paper from the bag when you're finished.)

Tip: You can reuse your wax paper for a purse or 2. If, however, you accidentally place 1 of the outer bag layers ink-side-out, the ink will stick to the wax paper—in that case, new wax paper should be used to prevent the ink from transferring back to the purse.

13 Extract the wax paper from the interior of the pocket.

14 Turn the bag right-side-out.

Fashion a Closure

15 Put the wax paper back inside the bag.

16 Take 2 of the handles you cut in step 3, trim them as needed, and twist them together lengthwise. You'll use these handles to create a loop inside the purse's flap through which a second set of handles can be tied.

Step 16: Twist two handles together.

17 To determine where the loop should be placed, lay the purse faceup, measure along the top of the flap to locate its center point, and then measure down about ½ in.

18 Form a loop with the twisted handles and iron each end of the loop to the inside of the flap such that the center of the loop straddles the point you measured in step 17. (Need we remind you to use wax paper?)

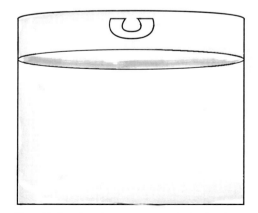

Step 18: Create a loop inside the bag's flap.

19 Repeat step 16 with 2 more handles.

20 Briefly apply the iron to the twisted handles to fuse them, again using wax paper to prevent the plastic handles from sticking to the iron.

21 Pinpoint the spot on the front of the bag where the loop will line up when the bag is closed and position the center point of the twisted handles accordingly.

22 Using just the tip of the iron (and wax paper), adhere the twisted handles to the front of the purse. Once the handles are adhered, you can close the bag by feeding 1 end of the twisted handles through the loop and tying the ends together.

Step 22: Adhere a set of handles to use as a tie.

Add a Handle

23 Lay the bottoms of the bags you cut in step 3 on top of each other. (Note that each bottom consists of 2 layers, meaning you are again working with 6 layers of plastic.)

24 Twist the stack of strips together.

25 Lay the purse facedown, with the flap raised.

26 Measure about 1½ in. in from the left and 1½ in. down from the top of the flap.

Note: If these measurements will result in a handle that is too short or too long, adjust them accordingly. The important thing is that the handle is centered on the purse.

27 Spread out the plastic on 1 end of the twisted strips and iron it to the back of the purse. (Spreading out the plastic on the end enables the handle to come into contact with a larger surface area, creating a stronger join and faster ironing.) Be sure to lay wax paper between any parts of the bag and handle that should not stick.

28 Repeat steps 26 and 27 on the right side of the purse.

Steps 23–28: Add a handle for the purse.

Tip: Optionally, decorate your purse with cutouts from other plastic bags, such as the nifty red circles used on the bag shown in the photo on page 72. Be sure to place each cutout ink-side-down before ironing to ensure that it sticks properly.

Ab Tab

Designer: Audra Evans

The average American consumes 5 cans of soda per day—which means you can accumulate the soda-can pop tabs necessary to construct this awesome belt in no time.

MATERIALS:

- LOTS of pop tabs (We used 80-ish.)
- 7mm-width ribbon (You'll need enough to wrap around your waist or hips twice, plus some extra to tie.)
- Scissors

Instructions

1. Cut 2 equal-length strips of ribbon, each long enough to wrap around your waist or hips once and tie into a bow.

2. Lay a pop tab faceup (i.e., with the smooth part of the tab facing upward) on your work surface.

3. Leaving enough ribbon on the left end to tie a bow, knot 1 length of ribbon to the top-left portion of the pop tab.

4. Knot the second length of ribbon to the bottom-left portion of the pop tab, again ensuring there's enough ribbon on the left end to tie a bow.

Steps 3–4: Knot the ends of the ribbon onto the tab.

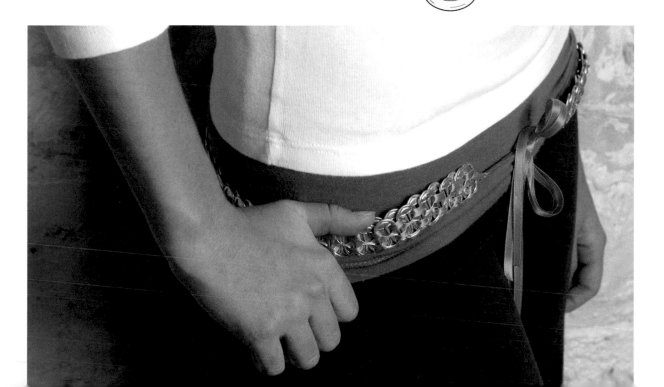

5 Lay a second pop tab (let's call it "Tab B") faceup on top of the one to which you have attached your ribbon (let's call it "Tab A"), with the left half of Tab B covering the right half of Tab A.

Step 5: The left half of Tab B should cover the right half of Tab A.

Tab A

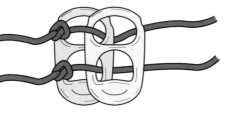

Tab B

6 Pull the top strip of ribbon through the top hole of Tabs A and B from front to back.

7 Pull the bottom strip of ribbon through the bottom hole of Tabs A and B from front to back.

Steps 6–7: Pull the strips of ribbon through both tabs from front to back.

8 Lay a new pop tab (let's call it "Tab C") under Tab B, adjacent to Tab A.

9 Draw the top ribbon through the top holes of Tab B and Tab C from back to front.

10 Draw the bottom ribbon through the bottom holes of Tab B and Tab C from back to front.

Tab A   Tab C   Steps 8–10: Add Tab C.

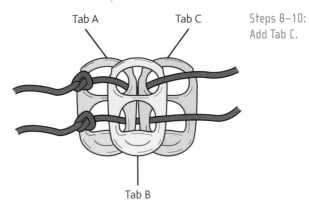

Tab B

11 Repeat steps 5–10, adding a new pop tab either above or below the last one added and weaving the ribbon either from front-to-back or back-to-front. Stop when the length of woven tabs is long enough to encircle your waist or hips, with enough ribbon on either end to tie a bow.

12 Knot the top length of ribbon to the upper-right portion of the last tab you added.

13 Knot the bottom length of ribbon to the bottom-right portion of the last tab you added.

The Refuse Refuge:

Projects for Around the House

5

Pop Art

Designer: Kate Shoup

You can upcycle your aluminum cans into any number of arty pieces—think picture frames, mirror frames, mosaics, signs, or address placards, as outlined here. Like the iPod holder, this project is a little tricky. But we think you'll love the end result. (Note that this placard is large enough to contain four digits; if your address is longer or shorter, you'll want to adjust accordingly.)

MATERIALS:

- 10 empty beverage cans (Six of these cans should be of one variety, 2 of a second variety, and the remaining 2 of a third variety. Look for cans in contrasting colors.)

- Tin snips

- Work gloves

- Rag

- Permanent marker (such as a Sharpie)

- Ruler

- Embroidery scissors

- Tracing paper

- Fine-point pen

- 1 piece of wood (Ours was 12 × 6 × ½ in.)

- 1 small package of nails (Be sure the nails are not too long; otherwise, they'll pierce the backside of the wood. Because our wood was ½ in. thick, we opted for nails that were ⁷/₁₆ in. long.)

- Hammer

- 2 sawtooth picture hangers

Instructions

Eviscerate Your Cans

1. Use your tin snips to cut the top and bottom ends off the can, such that you are left with an aluminum cylinder. (Remember: Unless you want to slice off a digit or two in the process, wear work gloves when cutting.)

2. Still using your tin snips and work gloves, cut the cylinder in a straight line lengthwise, resulting in an aluminum rectangle.

Note: I like to cut through the portion of the can that contains the nutritional information, as that's the least visually compelling part of the can.

3. Wipe the inside of the can with your rag to remove any droplets of soda, and flatten out the aluminum to the extent that it is possible by gently working it with your hands. When it's as clean and flat as possible, set it aside.

4. Repeat steps 1–3 on the remaining 9 cans.

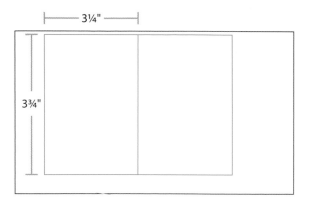

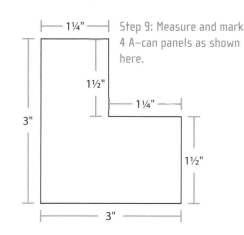

Step 6: Measure and mark 2 3¾ × 3¼-in. panels on the back of an A can.

Step 9: Measure and mark 4 A-can panels as shown here.

Shape the Aluminum

5   Organize the flattened aluminum by can type, placing the 6 matching cans (we'll call these "A") in one pile; the 2 matching cans (we'll call these "B") in a second pile; and the remaining 2 matching cans (let's call them "C") in a third pile.

6   Using your ruler and Sharpie, measure and mark 2 3¾ × 3¼-in. panels on the back of 1 of the A cans.

7   Using your embroidery scissors, carefully cut out the 2 panels.

8   Repeat steps 6 and 7 on the remaining A cans. When you're finished, you should have 12 3¾ × 3¼-in. panels.

9   Using your ruler and Sharpie, measure and mark the backs of 4 of the A-can panels you cut as shown here.

10 Using your embroidery scissors, carefully cut out the shapes you marked in step 9.

11 Using your ruler and Sharpie, measure and mark 2 3¼ × 3½-in. panels on the back of 1 of the B cans.

12 Using your embroidery scissors, carefully cut out the 2 panels.

13 Using your ruler and Sharpie, measure and mark 1 6½ × 3½-in. panel on the back of the remaining B can.

14 Using your embroidery scissors, carefully cut out the panel.

15 Lay your tracing paper over the first digit of your address and, using your fine-point pen, trace it.

Note: We generated the digits on pages 80–81 using a word processing program. The numbers shown are "actual size" because you are tracing them for this project. The font used is Rockwell Extra Bold, sized at 200 points. If you prefer a different font or size, then feel free to print your own sheet of digits.

16 Using your embroidery scissors, cut out the digit you traced.

17 Repeat steps 15 and 16 for the remaining digits of your address.

3 4

7 8

0

18 Lay 1 of the C cans facedown on your work surface.

19 Lay the tracing-paper cutout of the first digit of your address backward on the left side of the C can. (You place the digit backward so that it will be facing the correct direction when you cut it out and place the digit right-side-up.)

20 Using your Sharpie, trace around the tracing-paper cutout.

21 Lay the tracing-paper cutout of the second digit of your address backward on the remaining side of the C can.

22 Using your Sharpie, trace around the tracing-paper cutout.

23 Using your embroidery scissors, cut out both digits.

24 Repeat steps 18–23 with the remaining C can to cut out the last 2 digits of your address.

Prepare the Wood

25 Lay your wood piece horizontally on your work surface. Locate the center point of the left edge of the piece and the center point of the right edge of the wood piece, and, using your ruler as a straightedge, draw a line with your Sharpie from 1 point to the other.

26 Locate the center point of the top edge of the wood piece and the center point of the bottom edge of the wood piece, and, using your ruler as a straightedge, draw a line from 1 point to the other.

27 Draw a horizontal line across the wood piece that is 1¼ in. from the top edge.

28 Draw a horizontal line across the wood piece that is 1¼ in. from the bottom edge.

29 Draw a vertical line down the wood piece that is ¾ in. from the left edge.

30 Draw a vertical line down the wood piece that is 1 in. from the left edge.

31 Draw another vertical line down the wood piece that is 1½ in. from the left edge.

32 Draw another vertical line down the wood piece that is 2¾ in. from the left edge.

33 Draw a vertical line down the wood piece that is ¾ in. from the right edge.

34 Draw a vertical line down the wood piece that is 1 in. from the right edge.

35 Draw another vertical line down the wood piece that is 1½ in. from the right edge.

36 Draw another vertical line down the wood piece that is 2¾ in. from the right edge.

37 Draw a vertical line down the wood piece that is 1¾ in. to the left of the center vertical line.

38 Draw a vertical line down the wood piece that is 1¾ in. to the right of the center vertical line.

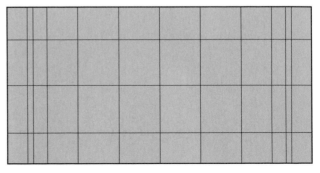

Steps 25–38: You'll use these lines as guides when you attach the aluminum panels.

Attach the Center Panels

39 Place the 6½ × 3½-in. panel in the center of the wood piece, aligning the left and right edges with the lines you drew in steps 32 and 36, respectively, and the top and bottom edges with the lines you drew in steps 27 and 28. Then use a hammer and nails to affix the panel to the board.

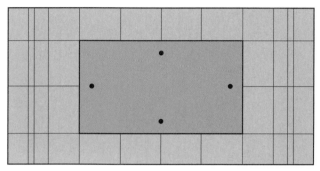

Step 39: Affix the large aluminum panel to the board.

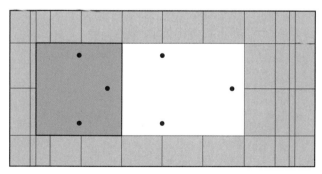

Step 40: Add the next panel.

40 Align the left and right edges of one of the 3¼ × 3½-in. B-can panels with the lines you drew in steps 30 and 37. (These lines are 1 in. from the left edge and 1¾ in. to the left of the center line, respectively.)

Then match up the top and bottom edges with the larger panel you just added. (Note that there will be about 1½ in. of overlap between the panel you're adding and the one you just added.) Then use a hammer and nails to affix the panel to the board.

41 Rotate the wood piece 180 degrees so that the panel you just added is now on the right side of the board and repeat step 40 to add another panel.

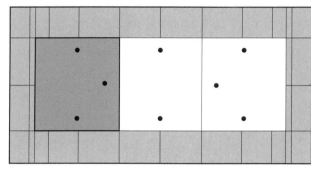

Step 41: Mirror the panel you added in step 40 on the other side of the board.

Attach the Border

42 It's time to attach the border. To begin, lay one of the 3¾ × 3¼-in. A-can panels horizontally along the bottom of the board, aligning it with the lines you drew in steps 37 and 38. (These lines are 1¾ in. to the left of the center line and 1¾ in. to the right of the center line, respectively.) It should slightly overlap the bottom of the large B-can panel you affixed to the middle of the board, and extend beyond the bottom of the board. Then use a hammer and nails to affix the new panel.

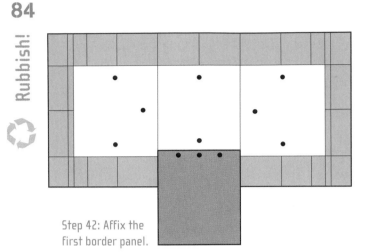

Step 42: Affix the first border panel.

43 Pull the bottom of the panel over the edge of the board and around to the backside of the wood. To ensure the crispest possible edge, try rolling your pen against the can as you pull it up and over the edge. Then use a hammer and nails to affix the panel to the backside of the wood.

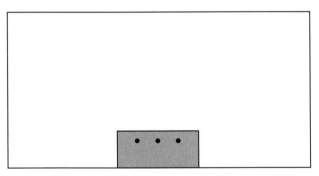

Step 43: Affix the panel to the backside of the wood.

44 With the wood piece faceup, rotate it 180 degrees so that the panel you just added is at the top. Then repeat steps 42 and 43 to add another panel.

45 Align the left edge of one of the 3¾ × 3¼-in. A-can panels with the line you drew in step 29 (this line is ¾ in. from the left edge of the board), matching up the top of the panel with the top of the one you just added. This new panel should slightly overlap both the bottom of panels above it and the left edge of the panel you just added, and should extend beyond the bottom of the board. Then use a hammer and nails to affix the panel to the board.

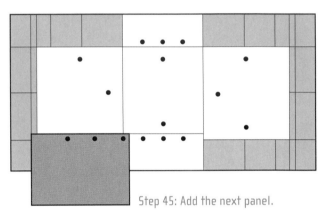

Step 45: Add the next panel.

46 Repeat step 43 to affix the bottom part of the panel to the backside of the board.

47 With the wood piece faceup, rotate it 180 degrees so that the panel you just added is at the top, and repeat steps 45 and 46 to add another panel.

48 Next, add a 3¾ × 3¼-in. A-can panel to the right half of the bottom border by following steps 45 and 46, this time aligning the panel with the line you drew in step 33 (the one that's ¾ in. from the right side of the board).

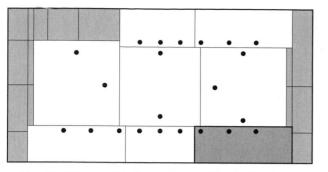

Step 48: Add a panel to the right side of the bottom border.

49 With the wood piece faceup, rotate it 180 degrees so that the panel you just added is at the top; then repeat step 48 to add another panel.

50 Lay 1 of the 3¾ × 3¼-in. A-can panels vertically along the left side of the board, aligning the top of the panel with the top of the center panels, and the right edge of the panel with the line you drew in step 31. (This line is 1½ in. from the left edge of the board.) The top of the panel should line up with the top of the center panels, and the left portion of the panel should extend beyond the left edge of the board. Then use a hammer and nails to affix the new panel.

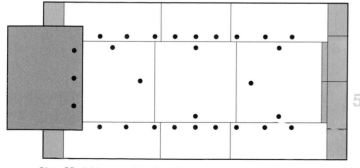

Step 50: Add a panel to the side.

51 Repeat step 43 to affix the left part of the panel to the backside of the board.

52 With the wood piece faceup, rotate it 180 degrees so that the panel you just added is on the right. Then repeat steps 50 and 51 to attach another panel.

53 Next, add the corners. To begin, place an L-shaped A-can piece in the lower-left corner, aligning it as shown, and use a hammer and nails to affix the new panel to the board.

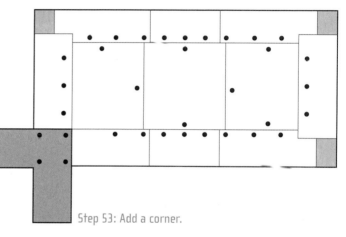

Step 53: Add a corner.

54 Pull the portion of the L-shape that is pointing downward over the edge of the board and around the backside of the wood. Again, to ensure the crispest possible edge, try rolling your pen against the can as you pull it up and over the edge. Then use a hammer and nails to affix it to the backside of the wood.

55 Repeat step 54 with the portion of the L-shape that is pointing to the left.

56 With the wood piece faceup, rotate it 90 degrees clockwise so that the corner you just added is in the top-left corner.

57 Repeat steps 53–56 3 times to add the remaining 3 corners.

Add the Digits

58 Arrange the address digits in the center portion of the board as desired, and use the hammer and nails to affix each digit to the board.

Add Sawtooth Picture Hangers

59 Determine where on the back of your board the sawtooth picture hangers should go. (We placed one 3 in. from the left edge and the other 3 in. from right edge, slightly below the folded-over panels.) Then use the hammer and nails to affix the hangers to the board.

You're So Negative

Designer: Tiffany Moreland

Even if you've embraced the digital camera age, odds are you have multiple shoeboxes stuffed with negatives stowed in the back of your closet. To create a new home for all those smiling faces, try constructing this fantastic photo-negative lampshade; we're positive you'll love the result.

MATERIALS:

- A pile of old negatives
- Scissors
- Sewing needle
- Thread

- Old lamp with lampshade (You'll fare best with a shade that's cylindrical in shape, but a flared one also works.)
- Low-wattage bulb

Instructions

1. Remove the fabric from the lampshade.

2. Thread your needle.

3. Knot the tail end of the thread around the hoop comprising the top of the lampshade frame.

4. Feed your needle through the top-left hole of the first negative you want to add.

Steps 5–6: "Sew" the first negative to the hoop.

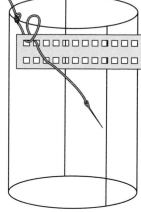

5. Wrap the thread around the hoop, and then pull the needle and thread through the next hole on the negative.

6. Repeat step 5 until only a few holes remain on the negative's top row. (For the sake of example, let's leave 3 holes open.)

7. To add a second negative, line up the 3 left-most holes in the second negative with the 3 right-most holes in the first one. The holes in the new negative should be lying over the holes on the existing one.

8. Pull the needle and thread through the first set of lined-up holes.

9. Wrap the thread around the hoop, and then pull the needle and thread through the next set of lined-up holes.

10. Repeat step 9 for the remaining set of lined-up holes.

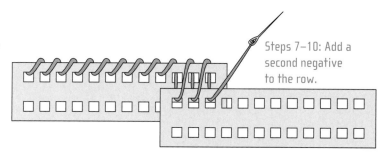

Steps 7–10: Add a second negative to the row.

11 Repeat steps 5 and 6 to attach the second negative to the top hoop.

12 Continue adding negatives to the top hoop as needed until you come back around to the first negative. (The number of negatives you add depends on the size of the hoop.) If necessary, cut the last negative you add to size.

Tip: If you run low on thread, tie off and start a new one as outlined in step 3, weaving through the negatives as needed to pick up where you left off.

13 After you've finished adding negatives to the top hoop, you're ready to start a new row of negatives. To begin, line up the bottom holes of a negative already sewn to the shade with the top holes of the negative you want to add. This time, however, don't lay the holes over each other as you did before.

Steps 13–16: Begin the second row.

14 Draw your needle and thread through the bottom-left hole of the negative on the existing row from back to front, and then through the top-left hole of the negative on the new row from front to back.

15 Draw your needle through the next hole along the bottom of the negative on the existing row from back to front and then through the next hole along the top of the negative on the new row from front to back.

16 Continue in this vein until only a few holes remain. (Again, for the sake of example, let's leave 3 holes.)

17 Adding a new negative to the second row is akin to adding a new negative to the first row. To begin, line up the 3 left-most holes in the new negative with the 3 right-most holes in the existing one. The holes in the new negative should be lying over the holes in the negative in the same row, but not over the holes in the negative in the row above. Then continue sewing as in steps 15 and 16 to attach the negative to the ones already on the hoop.

18 Continue adding rows in this fashion until the shade is covered.

Note: If the bottom row of negatives doesn't quite match up with the hoop comprising the bottom hoop of the shade's frame, fold the negatives in the row length-wise and attach them to the hoop by stitching through the bottom and top rows of holes in each negative.

19 Affix the shade to the lamp and switch it on.

Bottle It Up

Designers: Lisa Vetter and Paul Siefert

Look, no one's asking you to bottle up your emotions. For one, it's bad for you. Secondly, you'd be wasting a perfectly good bottle, which could be put to much better use as a wall vase. So take our advice and channel your feelings into this project; the substantial grinding, bending, and hammering required is sure to improve your mood.

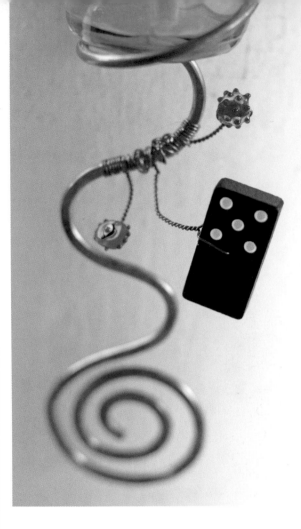

MATERIALS:

- A bottle
- Work gloves
- Grinder
- Needle nose pliers
- Large round nose pliers
- Bolt cutters
- Wire cutters
- 6-gauge copper wire

- 20-gauge copper wire
- Beads and misc. found objects (Think old pieces of jewelry, buttons, game pieces, etc.)
- Plenty of muscle

Optional

- Hammer
- Large anvil

Instructions

1 With your gloves on, use your bolt cutters to cut a 52-in. piece of 6-gauge copper wire. (After it's cut, coil the wire loosely to make it a bit easier to work with.)

2 Grind the ends of the copper wire to dull the sharp edges.

3 Using the large round nose pliers, coil one end of the wire into a spiral. Then form the wire above the spiral into a gentle S-shape.

4 Using your hands, shape another spiral above the S-shape, but at a 90-degree angle from the original spiral; this will support the bottom of bottle.

5 Place the base of bottle against the spiral and hand form the wire around the bottle to the top.

6 Using large round nose pliers, form yet another spiral at the top of the bottle.

7 Adjust the top spiral by hand to enable the bottle to hang flat against the wall.

Optional: Lay the bottom spiral on the anvil and use your hammer to beat it senseless. This adds texture.

8 Using your wire cutters, snip a 36-in. piece of 20-gauge copper wire.

9 Decide where you want to add beads to adorn the vase, and wrap about 3 in. of the copper wire to begin.

10 Extend the wire away from the piece and use the needle nose pliers to bend the wire at a right angle about 2–3 in. out.

11 Thread a bead (or other object) onto the wire, fold the wire over the bead, and twist the wire around the 2–3-in. stem you created in step 10 to secure it.

12 Repeat steps 10 and 11 to affix more objects, adding as much or as little adornment as desired.

Game Time

Designer: Kate Shoup

Game night. It's practically an American institution. Make sure to keep it that way with this upcycled game-board clock.

MATERIALS:

- 1 game board

- 12 game pieces

- Sturdy X-ACTO knife

- Spray adhesive (We used Krylon.)

- Drill (Make sure the bit is large enough to create a hole of adequate size to fit the clockwork piece through.)

- Clockwork piece (These are available at craft stores; alternatively, recycle the works from a clock you're not wild about.)

- Glue gun and glue sticks

- Ruler

- Fine-point marker

Instructions

1 After determining what portion of your game board should be used as the clock face, use your ruler and marker to mark it out.

2 Employing the ruler as a straightedge, use your X-ACTO knife to cut out the clock face.

3 Cut out a second piece of the game board that's the same size and shape as the clock face. This will serve as backing to strengthen the board.

4 Lay the clock facedown on your work surface.

5 Coat the backing with the spray adhesive.

6 Press the backing firmly onto the back-side of the clock face.

7 After letting the adhesive dry, use your ruler to locate the center point of the backside of the clock, marking it with your marker.

8 Drill through the clock's center point.

9 Following the manufacturer's instructions, affix the clockwork piece to the clock.

10 After determining where each hour on the clock should appear, use your glue gun and squirt a dot of hot glue on the bottom of a game piece.

11 Press the game piece onto the clock face at one of the hour positions.

12 Repeat steps 10 and 11 for the remaining 11 game pieces.

Turn Me On

Designer: Kate Shoup

Admit it: You have your share of really embarrassing paperbacks stashed in the back of your closet (think supercheesy fantasy novels, pulpy sci-fis, Fabio-friendly romances, etc.). But just because these books probably won't illuminate your mind doesn't mean you can't use them to help illuminate something else—such as your living room. How? By poaching their covers to act as switchplates for your light switches. (Note that the design shown here is a single-switch plate. If you need a switchplate for multiple switches, try using multiple covers.)

MATERIALS:

- 1 paperback romance novel (or other standard-size paperback)

- Cardboard box (We're talking the kind of box you use for shipping here.)

- 1 switchplate (You'll use this as a template to determine where the openings in your plate should go.)

- X-ACTO knife

- Ruler

- Fine-tip marker

- Scissors

- Small hole punch (This should create a hole that's the same size as the screws you'll use to screw on the switchplate.)

- Glue gun and glue sticks

- 8 small binder clips

- Small paintbrush

- Resin and hardener (We used EnviroTex Lite.)

- Small plastic cup or container

- Wooden stir stick

- 2 bamboo skewers

- Bowl

Instructions

Create the Cardboard Switchplate Frame

1 Using your ruler, measure your switchplate.

2 Using your ruler and marker, measure and mark on the cardboard box the dimensions of the switchplate. (Alternatively, lay the switchplate on the cardboard and simply trace around it.)

3 Using the X-ACTO knife, with the ruler acting as a straightedge, cut out the rectangle you measured and marked in step 2.

4 On the cardboard cutout, measure and mark a smaller rectangle whose edges are ½ in. from the edges of the cutout.

5 Using the X-ACTO knife, with the ruler acting as a straightedge, cut out the rectangle you measured and marked in step 4. The result is a cardboard frame.

Step 5: Cut out the inner rectangle to create a cardboard frame.

Prepare the Book Cover

6 Using your scissors, snip the romance novel's cover from the body of the book.

7 Lay the book cover facedown on your work surface.

8 Place the cardboard rectangle on the backside of the book cover and use your marker to trace around it.

Note: Be sure the area you're marking corresponds with the portion of the cover you want to appear on your switchplate.

9 On the backside of the book cover, measure and mark a larger rectangle whose edges are ⅝ in. outside the rectangle you just traced.

10 Using your scissors, cut out the larger rectangle.

11 Again, place the book cover facedown on your work surface. Then lay your switchplate facedown inside the rectangle you traced in step 8.

12 Using your marker, trace the cutout inside the switchplate where the light switch goes onto the backside of the book cover.

13 Mark the spot where each screw hole should go.

14 Using your X-ACTO knife, with the ruler acting as a straight-edge, create the rectangular cutout for the switch.

15 Using your hole punch, punch out the screw holes.

Steps 14–15: On the backside of the book cover, create the cutout for the switch and the screw holes.

16 Draw a line that starts in the top-left corner of the rectangle you drew in step 8 and travels up and to the right at a 45-degree angle.

17 Draw another line that starts at the top-left corner of the rectangle you drew in step 8, this time traveling down and to the left at a 45-degree angle.

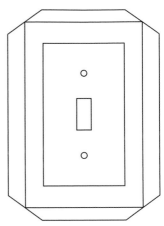

Steps 16–19: "Triangle off" the corners.

18 Cut along the lines you drew, excising the triangle that comprises the corner of the larger rectangle.

19 Repeat steps 16–18 on the remaining 3 corners.

Adhere the Cover to the Frame

20 Using your glue gun, squeeze a moderate amount of hot glue onto the cardboard frame.

21 Carefully press the cardboard frame sticky-side down onto the backside of the book cover, using the rectangle you traced in step 8 as a guide.

22 Again using the glue gun, squeeze a moderate amount of hot glue onto the top border of the cardboard frame.

23 Pull the top border of the book cover tightly over the edge of the cardboard and press it onto the hot glue.

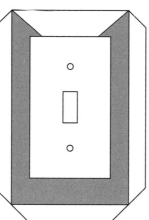

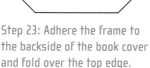

Step 23: Adhere the frame to the backside of the book cover and fold over the top edge.

Note: To ensure a crisper edge, try rolling your marker against the book cover as you pull it up and over the edge of the cardboard.

24 Use 2 binder clips to hold the edge of the book cover in place.

25 Repeat steps 22–24 on the remaining 3 edges.

Coat the Switchplate

26 After allowing adequate time for the glue to dry (give it a few hours), remove the clips from the book cover. Then use a wooden stir stick to mix the resin and hardener in a small plastic container, following the manufacturers' instructions carefully to ensure the resin will harden properly.

Note: Be sure to perform steps 26–32 in a well-ventilated area.

27 Place 2 bamboo skewers in parallel on a level, protected surface, and lay the switchplate faceup on the skewers. (This will prevent it from sticking to the surface.)

28 Using a small paintbrush, apply a layer of the resin/hardener compound to the edges of the switchplate. Don't use too much; otherwise, you'll wind up with drips, and the switchplate will stick to the skewers. (Don't forget to apply resin to the inner edges of the screw holes and switch cutout.)

29 Pour a small amount of the resin/hardener compound on the top surface of the switchplate. Use just enough to cover the top; don't let the compound drip down the sides.

30 Using the stir stick, spread the resin to distribute it evenly on the top of the switchplate.

31 Gently exhale on the surface of the switchplate to help eliminate bubbles in the resin.

32 Cover the switchplate with a bowl to prevent dust particles from settling on the resin and allow it to cure (this usually takes 3 days).

33 After the top surface of the switchplate has cured, flip the switchplate over and repeat steps 26–32 to coat the bottom surface.

Note: You may need to apply multiple coats of resin to obtain the desired shine on the cover.

Rock 'n' Bowl

Designer: Kate Shoup

Just because you've entered the era of digital music doesn't mean your LP collection is destined for doom. Why not turn those plastic platters into nifty bowls? They're great for serving popcorn, nuts, and other dry goods (avoid filling them with anything goopy; the label will be ruined, not to mention the leaking you'll experience thanks to the hole in the center of the disc), or for holding your change, keys, etc. By the way: Don't put this puppy in the microwave; it'll melt. Ditto in the dishwasher. To clean your LP bowl, just dampen a dish towel with warm, soapy water and run it along the edges.

MATERIALS:

- 1 LP record (Look for one with a colorful label.)
- Dish towel
- 1 cookie sheet
- Oven
- Oven mitts

- 1 bowl (This should be made of an oven-safe material. Any size will do; just be aware that using a larger bowl will result in a more shallow LP bowl and vice versa.)

Instructions

1. Preheat your oven to 200 degrees.

2. Dampen your dish towel with warm, soapy water and run it along the edges of your LP to clean it.

3. Place your bowl upside down on your cookie sheet.

4. Carefully place your LP (make sure it's had time to dry) on top of the upside-down bowl, centering the LP's label on the bottom of the bowl.

5. Slide the cookie sheet, bowl, and LP into the oven and "bake" it 3–5 minutes.

6. Using the oven mitts, extract the cookie sheet, bowl, and LP from the oven.

7. Still wearing the mitts, press the edges of the LP into a bowlish shape, fluting the edges, folding them over, or what have you.

Tip: You'll want to be quick here; as you work, the LP will cool, making it less pliable.

8 Let the LP cool; then carefully work it free of the oven-safe bowl.

Note: If you goofed—meaning your bowl turned out lopsided or otherwise flawed— just put the LP back in the warm oven until it's warmed back up and try again.

Creating a Better World, One Gift at a Time

6

Six-Pack

Designer: Kate Grenier

Downing an entire six-pack of beer can produce some unwanted results—think hangovers, blackouts, strangers in your apartment, etc. Assuming said six-pack involved bottles and not cans, however, you will also have six lovely bottle caps at your disposal—just the right number to craft these fantastic magnets.

MATERIALS:

- 6 bottle caps
- 6½-in. round magnets
- Glue (We like E-6000)
- 1 magazine
- Scissors
- Resin and hardener (We used EnviroTex Lite.)
- Small plastic cup or container
- Wooden stir stick
- Bowl

Instructions

1 Position the bottle caps concave-side down on your work surface

2 Squeeze a pea-size dollop of glue on the top of each bottle cap.

Tip: If you opted to use E-6000, give it 10 minutes or so to partially cure before proceeding to the next step.

3 On each bottle cap, press a magnetic button onto the glue, exerting enough pressure to establish full contact between the magnet and the bottle cap.

4 After allowing sufficient time for the adhesive to dry, flip the bottle caps over so they are concave-side up.

5 Flip through your magazine and locate 6 small, eye-catching images, letters, words, or phrases.

6 Use your scissors to cut the images, letters, words, or phrases into circles that are 1 in. in diameter.

7 Place each circle faceup inside a bottle cap.

8 In a well-ventilated area, use a wooden stir stick to mix the resin and hardener in a small plastic container, following the manufacturers' instructions carefully to ensure the resin will harden properly. You don't need a lot here—just enough to fill the bottle caps.

9 Pour resin into each bottle cap. It should completely cover the image in the cap.

10 Gently exhale on the surface to help eliminate bubbles in the resin.

11 Cover the bottle caps with a bowl to prevent dust particles from settling on the resin and allow it to cure. (This usually takes 3 days.)

Frame on You

Designer: Rebekah Seaman

During your last vacation, you captured *the* quintessential photo of your favorite traveling companion on the road. Why not construct a frame for it that features one of the pages from your road atlas? This project shows you how to do just that. You don't have to limit yourself to maps, however; architectural drawings, magazine spreads, encyclopedia pages—just about any type of ephemera can be used. (Note: Don't be intimidated by the number of steps here! The results are well worth it.)

MATERIALS:

- Map (Folded maps or pages from large atlases work equally well; alternatively, use some other type of ephemera, such as an architectural drawing or what have you.)
- Cardboard box
- Cereal box
- 3-in. ribbon
- 1 sheet newspaper
- Rubber cement
- Glue gun and glue sticks
- Pencil
- Ruler
- Scissors
- 6 art clamps or clothespins
- Sturdy X-ACTO knife
- Fine X-ACTO knife

Instructions

Prep the Frame

1 Using the sturdy X-ACTO knife, cut an 8 × 10-in. piece of cardboard from the cardboard box.

2 In the center of the 8 × 10-in. piece of cardboard, measure a 3½ × 5½-in. opening, marking the edges, using your pencil and ruler.

Note: Although this frame is designed to hold a 4 × 6-in. photo, cutting the opening a bit smaller than that ensures that none of the cardboard behind the photo will be visible.

3 Employing your ruler as an edger, use the sturdy X-ACTO knife to cut out the 3½ × 5½-in. opening.

4 Using your scissors, cut a 10 × 12-in. piece of newspaper.

5 Coat 1 side of the 8 × 10-in. piece of cardboard you cut in step 1 with rubber cement.

6 Lay the 8 × 10-in. piece of cardboard rubber-cement-side down on the newspaper such that a 1-in. border of newspaper appears around the cardboard.

7 After waiting 3–4 minutes for the rubber cement to dry, "triangle off" the corners of the newspaper. To begin, draw a line that starts at the top-left corner of the cardboard and travels up and to the right at a 45-degree angle.

8 Draw another line that starts at the top-left corner of the cardboard, this time traveling down and to the left at a 45-degree angle.

9 Cut along the lines you drew, excising the triangle that comprises the upper-left corner of the newspaper.

10 Repeat steps 7–9 on the remaining 3 corners.

11 Coat the top edge of the exposed cardboard with rubber cement.

12 Pull the top border of the newspaper tightly over the edge of the cardboard and press it onto the rubber cement.

Note: To ensure a crisper edge, roll your pencil against the newspaper as you pull it up and over the edge of the cardboard.

13 Repeat steps 11 and 12 on the remaining 3 edges.

Adhere the Map

14 Place your frame over your map, lining it up so the parts of the map you want visible will be on the frame.

Tip: If necessary, hold the frame and map up to the light for a better view of which map features will and will not appear on the frame.

15 With the frame and map lined up as desired, set them down carefully, and use a pencil on the backside of the map to trace the outline of the frame.

16 Using your ruler, measure an extra 1½ in. around the outline you drew in step 15, marking this new outline with your pencil.

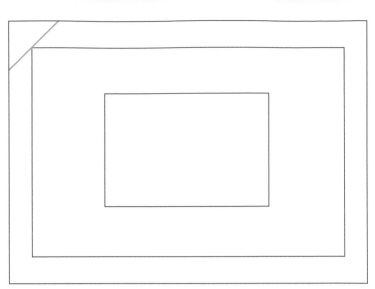

Steps 7–8: "Triangle off" the corners.

Step 12: Pull the newspaper over the edge of the cardboard.

17 Using your scissors, cut the outline you marked in step 16. The cut map should measure 13 × 15 in.

18 Coat the side of the frame that has been newspapered over in rubber cement.

19 Line up the frame with the outline you drew on the map in step 15 and press it firmly onto the map, rubber cement-side-down.

20 Flip the frame back over and roll your pencil over it to smooth out the map.

21 After allowing the rubber cement to dry (give it 4–5 minutes), repeat steps 7–10 to "triangle" the corners of the map.

22 Lay the frame map-side-down and, as you did with the newspaper, pull the top edge of the map up and over the edge of the frame, again rolling your pencil along the map as you pull it up and over the edge of the cardboard—but don't coat the edge of the frame with rubber cement just yet.

23 Repeat step 22 with the remaining 3 sides, still holding off on the rubber cement. The idea here is to prep the map to best adhere to the frame.

24 Coat the top edge of the frame with rubber cement.

25 Now pull the top border of the map over the edge of the frame and press it onto the rubber cement, again ensuring the crispest possible edge by rolling your pencil against the map as you pull it up and over the edge. Take special care to pull the corners in as tightly as possible.

26 Using your art clamps or clothespins, clamp down the middle and both corners.

27 Allow 5–7 minutes for the rubber cement to dry; then repeat steps 24–26 on the bottom edge of the frame.

28 After the rubber cement along the top and bottom edges of the frame has dried, repeat steps 24–26 on the left and right edges.

29 When the rubber cement along the left and right edges has dried, lay the frame facedown and, using your fine X-ACTO knife, cut a line from the top-left corner of the 3½ × 5½-in. opening to the bottom-right corner.

30 Repeat step 29, cutting from the top-right corner to the bottom-left corner.

31 Use your glue gun to coat the top triangular flap in hot glue.

32 Pull the coated flap tightly over the top edge of the opening and adhere it to the backside of the frame, clamping it into place with an art clamp or clothespin.

33 After allowing 5–7 minutes for the hot glue to dry, repeat steps 31 and 32 on the bottom flap.

34 After the top and bottom flaps have dried, repeat steps 31 and 32 on the left and right flaps.

Construct the Backing

35 Using the fine X-ACTO knife or sharp scissors, cut a 6 × 8-in. piece from the cereal box. This will be the backing to your frame.

36 Using your scissors, cut a 7 × 9-in. piece of map.

37 Coat the shiny side of the 6 × 8-in. piece of box in rubber cement, center it on the backside of the map you cut in step 36, and press it firmly into place.

38 After the rubber cement you used in step 37 dries (give it 3–4 minutes), repeat steps 7–12 on all 4 corners of the frame's backing.

39 Again, wait for the rubber cement on the backing to dry (allow 4–5 minutes). Then lay the frame facedown on your work surface, center the backing on the frame, and use your pencil to outline the backing.

40 Set the backing aside for a moment and, using your glue gun, squeeze a line of glue along the left, bottom, and right of the frame's opening, about ¼ in. from the edge.

Note: Do not put a line of glue around the top. This is where the photo will slide in.

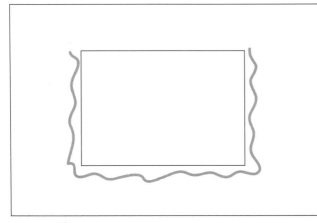

Step 40: Line the left, bottom, and right edge of the opening with glue.

41 Use your glue gun to squeeze a dot of glue on all 4 corners of the backside of the backing (that is, the side that is not covered by the map.

42 Using the outline you drew in step 39 as a guide, press the backing onto the back of the frame.

Add a "Hook"

43 Using your scissors, cut the edges of your 3-in. piece of ribbon at an angle.

44 Using your glue gun, squeeze a dot of glue onto the bottom edge of the ribbon.

45 Fold the ribbon in half short-ways and press the ends together.

46 After the glue dries, use your ruler and pencil to locate and mark the spot on the backside of the frame where you want to affix the ribbon hook.

47 Using your glue gun, squeeze a dot of glue on the back of the looped ribbon and firmly press it on the mark you made in step 46.

48 Let it all dry, slip in a picture, and hang your 100 percent recycled frame for all to see!

Do Not Pass Go

Designer: Kate Shoup

Just because your dog ate a few critical pieces of your Monopoly/Parcheesi/Chutes and Ladders/Bingo set doesn't mean the game should be tossed. Board games are chock-full of nifty cards and other printed fare that make great embellishments for handmade greeting cards, party invitations, and the like. (Note that this type of ephemera can also be fashioned into kick-ass magnets; just stick it onto an adhesive-backed magnet sheet and trim off the edges.)

MATERIALS:
- 1 board game card
- 1 blank greeting card made of recycled paper (Ours was 3 x 5 in.)
- 1 matching envelope
- Spray adhesive (We like the kind made by Krylon.)
- Paper towel

Instructions

1 Spritz a small amount of spray adhesive onto the back of the board game card.

Note: You don't need much in the way of adhesive—in fact, the less you can get away with using, the better. Otherwise, when you press the game board card onto the front of the blank greeting card, the excess adhesive will ooze out from around the edges.

2 Decide where you want the board game card to appear on the greeting card and press it on.

3 If any excess adhesive oozes out from behind the board game card, use the paper towel to remove it.

Dip Lit

Designer: April Richardson

So you've consumed an entire tin of bean dip. Fear not: You can cancel out the aromas that are sure to ensue with this lovely scented candle.

Instructions

1 Preheat your oven. Opt for the lowest temperature possible—i.e., the "warm" setting.

2 Thoroughly wash and dry the inside of the tin, taking care to avoid messing up the paper label on the outer part of the container.

MATERIALS:

- 1 empty bean-dip tin (It doesn't have to be a bean dip tin. Other types of tins work just as well.)

- 1 clean glass jar

- used candle bits

- cookie sheet

- oven

- wick adhesive (We used Bluestik Mold Sealer by DAP; it's a type of putty that's designed to adhere to metal molds.)

- 1 wick (We like the pretabbed votive kind.)

- oven mitt

- scissors

3 Break up your candle bits into small pieces and place them in the glass jar.

Note: We're big fans of mixing and matching scents from multiple candles.

4 Place the glass jar on a cookie sheet and put it in your warm oven until the wax is completely melted. (This can take as long as 30 minutes or so.)

5 Put a spot of wick adhesive in the center of the bean-dip tin.

6 Firmly press the metal base of the wick onto the wick adhesive.

7 Using your oven mitt, remove the hot jar of liquefied wax from the oven and pour almost all of it into the tin.

8 As the wax cools, it will cave in a bit in the center; when it does, pour the last bit of wax into the center of the tin.

Tip: Pour the last bit of wax in after the candle has set up a bit—i.e., when a skin has begun to develop on the top. Don't wait too long, though, or you will have 2 very distinct wax layers.

9 Let the candle sit overnight in order for the wax to fully set.

10 Trim the wick so that it's about ¼ in. tall.

College Bound

Designer: Michael Dittman

When college professor Michael Dittman discovered that the paper his students so conscientiously tossed in recycling bins on campus was ultimately dumped along with the rest of the trash, he did what any Dumpster-diving tree-hugger would do. He launched a paper-rescue operation, gathering up the discarded sheets and binding them clean-side-up into notebooks bound with cardboard from such items as cereal boxes, beer cases, etc.

MATERIALS:

- Cardboard (Think cereal boxes, beer cases, etc.)

- Paper (Any type will do, but obviously sheets with one clean side that are otherwise doomed for the trash are best.)

- Paper cutter (Use an arm cutter with a cutting length of about 15 in.)

- Pencil

- Sturdy X-ACTO knife

Optional

- Binding machine

- Double-loop wire binding

- Wire cutters

- Needle nose pliers

Note: If you only intend to assemble, say, a dozen or so notebooks per year, your best bet is to visit your local copy store or mega office store and pay to have them bound. If, on the other hand, you really want to crank these notebooks out, then you might want to spring for a binding machine and double-loop wire binding. In that case, you'll also need to have some wire cutters and needle nose pliers handy.

Instructions

1 Using your X-ACTO knife, cut 2 pieces of cardboard for use as the front and back covers.

2 Slide the front cover into the paper cutter and trim it down to the desired size, taking care to trim inside any corner creases.

3 Using a pencil, lightly trace the measurements of the trimmed front cover to the inside of the back cover.

4 Slide the back cover into the paper cutter and trim it so that it is the same size as the front cover. (Don't panic if they're not *exactly* the same size; no one will notice or care.)

5 Decide how many sheets of paper you want your notebook to include, taking into account that a large book (e.g., cereal box size) looks odd with less than 20 pages, and a small book (think bandage box) looks pretty portly with more than 50 pages. For an average-sized book, we usually use about 60 pages.

6 Hand the front and back covers and the paper that goes in between to the person behind the counter at the copy store and ask him/her to bind it for you.

Alternatively, bind it yourself, following the instructions provided with your binding machine.

Note: If you opt for the latter, don't force matters; if your book is too big, remove some sheets and try again. Also, make sure that all your sheets are facing the same way—i.e., clean side up—before you start poking holes in them. After you've punched the necessary holes in the paper and covers, thread your wire binding through, cut the wire to length, and crimp the edges a little so they don't cut your crafty little hands.

Brut Strength

Designer: Terry Border

Courage in a bottle: It'll incite even the most cowardly among us to try things we shouldn't, including various feats of strength. In homage to this, we present this wire figure, fashioned from corks and bottle caps. (Don't let the number of steps intimidate you; you'll love the results.) For safety's sake, consider wearing protective glasses while attempting this project; you'll find they're more effective than beer goggles against accidentally poking yourself in the eye with wire.

MATERIALS:

- 2 corks
- 8 bottle caps
- 1 chopstick
- Several feet of 20-gauge galvanized wire
- Wire cutters

- Needle nose pliers
- Round nose pliers
- Pencil
- Drill (Make sure your bit is large enough to create a hole to accommodate the chopstick.)

Instructions

Form the Head

1 Using your wire cutters, cut a 1½-ft. length of wire.

2 Grasping the wire with your needle nose pliers, push it through 1 of the corks from top to bottom, pulling it until half the wire sticks out each end. This cork will be the figure's head.

3 Pull the top half of the wire up and over the top of the head and, using your needle nose pliers, form a backward L-shape.

4 Using your round nose pliers, form a small loop. This will be the figure's right eye. (It's the figure's right eye, but it's on your left.)

5 Form another loop to create the figure's left eye (on your right).

6 Bring the wire back to the center of the figure's face and bend it toward you at a 90-degree angle to form the bridge of the figure's nose.

7 Guide the wire around the stems of the round nose pliers to create the rest of the figure's nose and mouth.

8 Draw the wire over the bottom of the cork (i.e., the figure's chin) and wrap it several times around the wire that's emerging from the underside of the cork to create the neck.

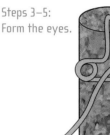

Steps 3–5:
Form the eyes.

Steps 6–7:
Form the nose and mouth.

9   Using your wire cutters, cut the excess from the portion of the wire you used to form the figure's facial features, but leave the wire that's emerging from the underside of the cork in place.

10 Cut a 1-in. length of wire.

11 Form the wire into a C-shape.

12 Press the ends of the wire into the right side of the cork; this is the figure's right ear.

13 Repeat steps 10–12 to add the figure's left ear.

Construct the Torso

14 Grasp the wire that's emerging from the underside of the cork with your needle nose pliers and push it through the remaining cork from top to bottom to create the figure's torso.

15 Draw the wire from the bottom of the torso along the backside of the cork, where the figure's spine would be, and then wrap it several times around the figure's neck to reinforce it.

16 Using your wire cutters, cut the excess from the wire you used to form the spine and reinforce the neck.

Create the Arms

17 Cut a 1-ft. length of wire.

18 Grasping the wire with your needle nose pliers, push it through the cork torso, near the top, from left to right, pulling it until half the wire sticks out each end. This wire will become the figure's arms.

19 Create a medium-sized loop at each shoulder joint.

20 Create a larger loop at each elbow joint.

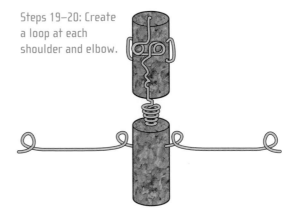

Steps 19–20: Create a loop at each shoulder and elbow.

21 Angle both arms upward, so that they are raised above the figure's head.

Note: Do not cut the excess wire from the arms quite yet. You'll need it later to form the figure's wrist.

22 Cut a 2-ft. length of wire.

23 Starting from behind the figure, feed the right end of the wire through the figure's left shoulder loop (i.e., the loop on your right).

24 Again starting from behind the figure, feed the left end of the wire through the figure's right shoulder loop (i.e., the loop on your left). The center point of the wire should be aligned with the cork.

25 Create a curve in the wire at its center point, bringing it up and over the top of the cork comprising the figure's torso and nestling it behind the figure's neck.

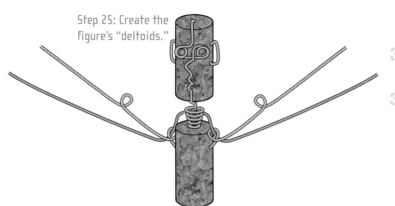

Step 25: Create the figure's "deltoids."

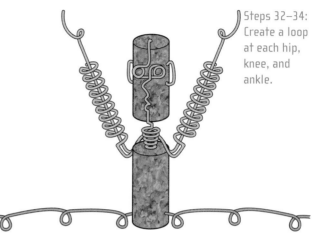

33 Create a large-ish loop at each knee joint.

34 Create a large-ish loop at each ankle joint.

Steps 32–34: Create a loop at each hip, knee, and ankle.

26 Lay your pencil against the wire comprising the figure's left arm (i.e., the arm on your right) and wrap the wire you fed through the shoulder loop around it several times to create a spiral shape.

27 When you reach the loop you formed to create the figure's elbow, feed the spiraled wire through it and then form the spiraled wire into a loop to attach it to the elbow loop.

28 Using your wire cutters, cut the excess wire from the spiraled piece.

29 Repeat steps 26–28 on the figure's right arm (i.e., the arm on your left).

Note: You'll finish the figure's arms, attaching them to the chopstick barbell, in a moment.

Form the Legs

30 Cut a 2-ft. length of wire.

31 Grasping the wire with your needle nose pliers, push it through the cork torso, near the bottom, from left to right, pulling it until half the wire sticks out each end. This wire will become the figure's legs.

32 Create a large-ish loop at each hip joint.

35 Angle both legs downward.

36 Cut a 2-ft. length of wire.

37 Pull the wire through the loop at the figure's left hip (i.e., the loop on your right) until its center point is inside the loop.

38 Bend the wire in half, draw it around the backside of the cork, and feed both ends through the loop at the figure's left hip (i.e., the loop on your right).

39 Lay your pencil against the wire comprising the figure's left leg (i.e., the leg on your right) and wrap one end of the wire you fed through the hip loop around it several times to create a spiral shape.

40 When you reach the loop you formed to create the figure's knee, feed the spiraled wire through it and then form the spiraled wire into a loop to attach it to the knee loop.

41 Using your wire cutters, cut the excess wire from the spiraled piece.

42 Pull the remaining half of the wire around the front of the cork torso and feed it through the loop at the figure's right hip (i.e., the loop on your left).

43 Repeat steps 39–41 to add a spiral to the remaining leg.

44 Cut a 1-ft. length of wire.

45 Feed the wire through the spiral you created around the figure's left leg (i.e., the leg on your right), looping one end of it around the first spiral near the figure's hip to attach it.

46 Feed the wire through the loop at the knee to the ankle, forming a loop to attach it there.

47 Work the wire you used to create the figure's legs in steps 39–43 to form the figure's heel, the blade of his foot, and the front half of the foot, ending by creating a loop or 2 to represent the big toe.

Tip: Give your figure big feet so you can balance him easily.

48 Using your wire cutters, snip the excess from the big toes.

49 Work the wire you added in steps 45 and 46 to create the inner portion of the foot, drawing it through the loops you created in step 47, and then wrapping it around the front half of the foot to create toes.

Steps 47–49: Construct the foot.

50 Using your wire cutters, snip the excess.

51 Repeat steps 44–50 on the remaining leg.

Add the Weight Bar

52 Cut a 1-ft. piece of wire.

53 Feed the wire through the spiral you created around the figure's left arm (i.e, the arm on your right) in steps 26–28, looping one end of it around the first spiral near the figure's shoulder to attach it.

54 Place the chopstick against the wire about 1½ in. beyond the elbow loop; then wrap the wire around the chopstick 4 times to create fingers, about 2 in. from the right end of the chopstick.

55 Using your wire cutters, cut the excess wire from the figure's hand.

56 Cut a 6-in. length of wire.

57 Loop 1 end of the wire to the figure's left elbow loop (i.e., the elbow loop on your right).

58 Create a large loop under the fingers, abutting the bottom edge of the chopstick, to form the palm of the hand.

59 Bring the wire up against the chopstick to form the thumb.

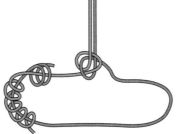

Steps 54–59: Construct the figure's hand.

60 Using your wire cutters, cut the excess wire from the thumb.

61 Grasp the excess wire from the figure's left arm (i.e., the arm on your right) with your needle nose pliers and wrap it several times around the wires that comprise the figure's hand to form the wrist.

62 Using your wire cutters, snip the excess wire from the figure's wrist.

63 Repeat steps 52–62 to finish the figure's other arm.

64 Drill a hole in the center of each bottle cap.

65 Feed 4 bottle caps onto the right end of the chopstick, prodding them up against the figure's fingers and arranging them in pairs of 2 that face each other.

66 Cut a 6-in. length of wire.

67 Wrap the wire around the chopstick just to the right of the bottle caps to secure them in place.

68 Using your wire cutters, trim the excess.

69 Repeat steps 65–68 to finish the remaining side.

Reduce, Reuse, Regift

Designer: Addie Panveno

You agonized over finding the perfect Earth-friendly gift for your beloved; you can't very well wrap it up in paper that will be immediately pitched. Instead, try fabricating a fetching gift box using food containers and leftover crafty bits. For an even greater impact, encourage your loved one to reuse the box—preferably to give a gift to *you*.

MATERIALS:

- 1 dry, clean food container with lid (A coffee tin or oatmeal container works well. If you can, opt for a container that has a lip around the top and/or bottom of the container; the lip can help keep the paper you apply to the container snug, and can also prevent the lid from catching on the paper.)

- Measuring tape

- Leftover paper (Think wrapping paper, origami paper, vintage wallpaper, old greeting cards, etc.)

- Craft studio leftovers (We used mismatched buttons, bits of ribbon, scraps of fabric, and the like.)

- Scissors

- Rubber cement (Note that this type of adhesive works beautifully on most containers, but may not adhere to some plastics. Assess your container to determine what type of bonding agent will yield the best result.)

- Glue gun and glue sticks

Optional

- Hole punch

Instructions

1 If your food container has a removable label, take it off as best you can.

2 Measure the container to determine its height and circumference.

Note: If your container has a lip around the top and/or bottom, do not include the lip when you measure.

3 Cut a strip of paper that is as tall as the container, and as long as the circumference of the container plus a couple of inches. (This will allow some overlap for anchoring the paper in place.)

4 Coat the container in rubber cement, applying the paper as you go. For best results, adhere the middle of the strip of paper to the container first, working around both sides; this prevents the formation of bubbles and gaps, and enables you to line up the paper more easily all the way around.

5 When you reach the ends of the paper, glue the shorter end to the container.

6 Overlap the shorter end with the longer end, securing it with hot glue from the glue gun.

7 With the base paper in place, you're ready to run wild. One approach is to apply more paper in layers to create a collaged look; alternatively, affix a wide ribbon to create a fresh, modern style. For added interest, use your glue gun to adhere bottle caps, buttons, or even old watch gears.

Tip: Avoid getting too specific with your decoration. Tacking on a picture of Grandma will sure tickle her fancy, but unless she gives gifts to herself, she probably will not reuse the box.

8 If you like, try decorating the lid. One approach is to use your glue gun to attach a big ribbon bow, buttons, or other doodads. Alternatively, use a hole punch to pierce the lid and attach paper flowers or decorative brads.

9 In lieu of store-bought tissue paper, stuff the box with thin strips of leftover paper (you can even fashion your own "zippies," strips of leftover cardstock or paper folded accordion style) or leftover fabric.

Note: If you have a paper shredder, you can run your junk mail through it to create stuffing for your box. If the results are too bland, try shredding pages from colorful magazines or catalogs.

About the Designers

April Alden   Artist and designer April Alden of Rosewebs lives in the Pacific Northwest. A welder by trade, Alden, who earned her Bachelor of Fine Arts in sculpture, is also a seamstress extraordinaire who particularly enjoys creating objects from reclaimed materials, noting that "Objects that survive our throw away culture are appealing in that most would deem them obsolete."

Terry Border   After obtaining his B.F.A. in photography from Ball State University, Indianapolis resident Terry Border launched a career in commercial photography, shooting such diverse and exciting products as ironing boards and cremation urns. In 1992, however, he switched careers, baking bread for a local supermarket in order to be home when his daughter finished school each day. As an added bonus, this work situation gave Terry (who describes his wife as "patient") time to pursue his love of art by fashioning wire sculptures and narrative scenes out of wire and whatever else he found lying around the house. Terry has since attracted a cultlike following on the Internet, thanks to his blog "Bent Objects" (www.bentobjects.blogspot.com).

Allison Brideau and **Melissa Mazgaj**   Allison Brideau and Melissa Mazgaj, who hail from New Brunswick, Canada, are the force behind Born Again Purses. Born crafters, best friends Brideau and Mazgaj developed their craft skills under the watchful eye of their mothers and other family members. Sisters in crafts, if not by blood, Brideau and Mazgaj pride themselves on creatively constructing purses with little or no waste. To view their purses and other items, search for their seller name, bornagainpurses, on Etsy.com. Goods by Born Again Purses are also available at www.bayoffundystore.com.

Roxane Cerda Roxane Cerda dabbles in dozens of crafts. Because she can't stay focused on one thing for long, she has become a Jacqui of all trades, master of none. Nonetheless, when she does whip up something spiffy, she loves to share and hopes you enjoy her project. Roxane began to craft ages ago, and has only looked back from time to time to ensure she's not trailing bits of string and dropping beads all over the place.

Michael Dittman Michael Dittman is the author of *Jack Kerouac: A Biography, Masterpieces of The Beat Generation* (Greenwood Press, 2004) and the novel *Small Brutal Incidents* (Contemporary Press, 2006). When not crafting with other people's garbage and selling the results on Etsy.com, Dittman runs the arts and culture blog venangago-go (venangago-go.blogspot.com). He lives, writes, teaches, and creates in Northwestern Pennsylvania.

India Evans High-school student and North Carolina resident India Evans's artistic interests include modern art, photography, clothing reconstruction, screen-printing, and making jewelry. She loves bright colors and finds inspiration for new projects from all around. When not studying or creating, Evans enjoys cooking, hanging out with friends, listening to music, and going out.

Andrea Glick-Zenith For artist Andrea Glick-Zenith, recycling neat bits has always been a passion. An official paper hoarder, whose collection of scraps delights her cats on a daily basis, Glick-Zenith also makes jewelry and graphics, writes senryu poetry, and runs the Wisconsin Street Team on Etsy.com. Visit Glick-Zenith's Etsy store at ZenithJade.Etsy.com to see her latest handmade creations; to comment on them (or send cat jokes), contact her at zenithjade@yahoo.com.

Kate Grenier Montana native Kate Grenier, whose interest in crafting was sparked by her woodworking father, blends handcrafting techniques to create pieces that can be found in boutiques nationwide. Recycling and reusing are integral parts of Grenier's work, which ranges from found bottle caps transformed into magnets to elegant accent tables bounded by poetry. A current resident of Portland, Oregon, Grenier, a graduate of UCLA, "explores ways for art to become useful and for useful objects to become art." To see Grenier's work, visit www.kategrenier.com, or contact her at creations@kategrenier.com.

Debby Grogan A native of Staten Island, New York, Debby Grogan has spent the last 28 years in south Florida because, as she says, "Snow sucks." In addition to launching Devon Ryan Designs, Grogan runs her own baby-shower and party-favor business from the home she shares with her husband, Kenton, and her son, Ryan. (Daughter Devon has since flown the coop to attend college.) Grogan's entrée into upcycling was sparked by her daughter's collection of *Rolling Stone* magazines, which she fashioned into bags; since then, she has expanded her reuse repertoire to include bowls, candles, clocks, and bags. Find Grogan's upcycled (and other) wares at www.devonryandesigns.com.

Yvonne Hoyer A lifelong crafter, Yvonne Hoyer (who, according to her grandparents, was always the most creative child in the family) spent her youth in Germany hunting for unique stones to paint or collect. These days, she's perpetually on the lookout for unique beads and other supplies to make her jewelry. Besides designing jewelry, she also remodels vintage furniture and has recently begun working with mosaics. Hoyer lives in Germany with her American husband on a U.S. Army base. Find more of Hoyer's work at her Etsy shop (www.justagirl27.etsy.com).

Mark Kirk and **Heather MacFarlane** Mark Kirk, a culinary graduate, and Heather MacFarlane, a fine arts graduate, met while fighting over a plastic chicken at a Mardi Gras parade. (Mark won.) Not long after this clashing-color matchup, they formed UP/Unique Products, known for funky lighting and housewares fashioned from New Orleans castoffs. In 1999, Kirk and MacFarlane opened their showroom/gallery, Upstairs, at 2038 Magazine Street, New Orleans, to showcase and sell their eccentric artwork. The duo's ever-expanding portfolio now includes event planning/décor, costume consultation, and alternative culinary creations, with a client roster that includes MTV, The Ogden Museum of Southern Art, The Museum of Natural History, National Galleries of Scotland, Golden Nugget Casino, HGTV, and many more throughout the United States, Canada, and Europe. When not Dumpster-diving, Kirk and MacFarlane love to hang out with their dog Dixie and play croquet, enjoying the "never a dull moment" city of New Orleans.

Tiffany Moreland Tiffany Moreland, who earned her B.F.A. in graphic design from Shepherd University, lives in the eastern panhandle of West Virginia. In her spare moments late at night and on weekends, Tiffany crafts trinkets and treasures from everyday items, including her trademark record-adaptor earrings, and does a brisk and well-received business on Etsy (tinsil.etsy.com). She also enjoys classic rock, yard sales, flea markets, and tomato soup with grilled cheese. Beyond all this, Tiffany's greatest achievement is the long, happy life of Jimmy, the world's most excitable goldfish.

Mike Mossey Mike Mossey is a designer, tinkerer, repair artist, and musician currently living in Tampa, Florida. Although repairing machinery and old buildings takes up most of the week, Mike also finds time to dismantle and repurpose old parts for use in jewelry and sculpture. Mike founded Fuzzy Space Outpost (www.fuzzyspaceoutpost.com) in 2000 with wife Meli (melimade.com), where they offer their wares.

Melissa Nappi Fiber artist Melissa Nappi has been making things for as long as she can remember, and loves to spin, knit, felt, and dye yarn and fiber. Always trying out new ideas and fibers, Nappi also writes knitting patterns. In her spare time, Melissa likes flying, skiing, hiking, kayaking, biking, camping, reading, ceramics, and playing video games. She is a master of Connect Four and rocks at Mario Kart. Visit Nappi at her online shop: rainydayart.etsy.com.

Addie Panveno Thirty-year old freelance writer, photographer, artist, and nomad Addie Panveno finds inspiration in change. Although she calls Newport, Kentucky, home, she has lived all over the country, with each city adding something to her artistic style. Appalled by the amount of waste created by old-school crafting, Panveno began to focus on using found, secondhand, and recycled items, making everything from jewelry to furniture. She loves to experiment, always trying something new. You can find her at epositive.etsy.com.

April Richardson April Richardson is an editorial assistant at a magazine by day and a stand-up comedy connoisseur by night. A recent transplant from Atlanta, Georgia, to Los Angeles, Richardson is disappointed that she has not yet met George Clooney. At age 14, Richardson made her first zine (way back in the pre-readily available-Internet days of 1993) and was immediately hooked. Besides zines and candles, April also likes to make 1-inch buttons, silkscreen T-shirts, coil bind notebooks (also made from recycled materials), and design covers for the wonderful mix tapes she makes. She's an avid Morrissey enthusiast and will probably high-five or hug you (or both!) soon after meeting. You can see her stuff at emotionlotion.org.

Rebekah Seaman

Rebekah Seaman is the artistan behind Ship by RLS frames. A crafter and avid recycler, Seaman sells her 100-percent recycled frames online at Etsy. com, as well as at various stores in the metro Boston area—although she pays the bills working in the field of gerontology. When not crafting or working, Seaman collects Pez, plays ice hockey (she played in college), and reads nightly. She lives in Jamaica Plain, Massachusetts, with her dog, George.

Paul Siefert and Lisa Vetter

The work of Paul Siefert and Lisa Vetter is inspired by the natural world and is in response to our throw-away society. The found objects they collect tell the stories of bygone travels and miscalculated gifts, and can be a historical reminder of previous generations. By creatively recycling these "treasures" with other media, Vetter and Siefert both offer a new story to an old item and challenge the viewer to observe these everyday items in a completely different way. Vetter and Siefert live and work at "The Art Farm," their restored 1860 farm studio and home in Spencerville, Indiana.

Allison Strine

Sometimes Allison Strine writes in the third person. When she does, this is what she says: By day, Allison Strine is a happy artist whose irrepressible creations have won awards and appeared in artsy magazines and craftsy books. At night she's a not-very-good cook, a wife to a left-brained husband, and a tucker-inner of two glorious children.

Shannon Wenisch

Born and raised in rural Rhode Island, Shannon Wenisch was bitten by the crafting bug at a very early age. When most kids were selling lemonade on the sidewalk, she had an origami stand to sell her handmade creations at the end of her driveway. She graduated from University of Rhode Island with a B.A. in English and has held a variety of jobs, from slinging coffee to banking and customer service, none of which has been as fulfilling as creating with her own two hands. Always eager to learn, Shannon is self-taught in many areas of crafty expertise. Nowadays, you can find her in her studio making jewelry and other handmade crafts to sell online. Shannon resides in Pittsburgh, Pennsylvania, with two cats and her husband, Thomas.

About the Author

Kate Shoup has written more than a dozen books on a wide range of topics, including *Not Your Mama's Beading, Not Your Mama's Stitching, The Agassi Story, iPhone VISUAL Quick Tips, Webster's New World English Grammar Handbook,* and more. She has also co-written (and starred in) an independent feature film and formerly worked as the sports editor for her local alternative weekly paper. When not writing or crafting, Kate loves to ski (she was once nationally ranked), ride her motorcycle, and read—and she plays a mean game of 9-ball. Kate lives in Indianapolis with her daughter and their dog.

Index